THE GRASS HARP

Also by Truman Capote

THE GRASS HARP (novel)
LOCAL COLOR
A TREE OF NIGHT AND OTHER STORIES
OTHER VOICES, OTHER ROOMS

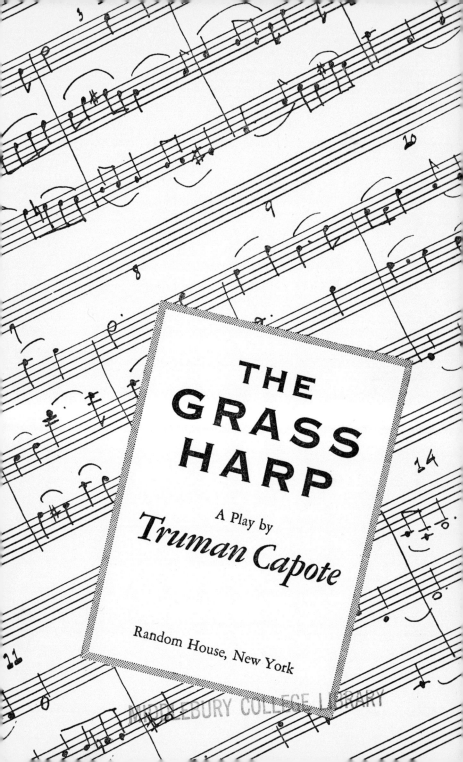

THE GRASS HARP

A Play by

Truman Capote

Random House, New York

FIRST PRINTING

COPYRIGHT, 1952, BY TRUMAN CAPOTE

ALL RIGHTS, INCLUDING THE RIGHT OF
REPRODUCTION IN WHOLE OR IN PART IN ANY FORM,
ARE RESERVED UNDER INTERNATIONAL AND
PAN-AMERICAN COPYRIGHT CONVENTIONS.

PUBLISHED IN NEW YORK BY RANDOM HOUSE, INC., AND
SIMULTANEOUSLY IN TORONTO, CANADA, BY
RANDOM HOUSE OF CANADA, LIMITED.

LIBRARY OF CONGRESS CATALOG CARD NUMBER: 52-8665

MANUFACTURED IN THE UNITED STATES OF AMERICA

For Saint-Subber
in deep appreciation

THE GRASS HARP was first presented by Saint-Subber in association with Rita Allen at the Martin Beck Theatre, New York City, on March 27, 1952, with the following cast:

(In Order of Appearance)

CATHERINE CREEK	*Georgia Burke*
COLLIN TALBO	*Johnny Stewart*
DOLLY TALBO	*Mildred Natwick*
VERENA TALBO	*Ruth Nelson*
DR. MORRIS RITZ	*Jonathan Harris*
THE REVEREND'S WIFE	*Susan Steell*
THE REVEREND	*Ralph Hertz*
THE BARBER	*Sterling Holloway*
THE BAKER'S WIFE	*Gertrude Flynn*
THE POSTMASTER	*Jay Barney*
THE SHERIFF	*Val Dufour*
JUDGE CHARLIE COOL	*Russell Collins*
THE CHOIR MISTRESS	*Jane Smith*
BIG EDDIE STOVER	*Anthony McGrath*
BROPHY	*Jules Racine*
SAM	*Larry Robinson*
MAUDE RIORDAN	*Lenka Peterson*
MISS BABY LOVE DALLAS	*Alice Pearce*

Directed by Robert Lewis

Music by Virgil Thompson

Scenery and costumes by Cecil Beaton

SCENES

ACT ONE

Scene I—The Talbo House. A Sunday afternoon late in September.

Scene II—The town. The following morning

Scene III—An autumn wood. The same day

ACT TWO

Scene I—The wood. Early the following morning and that night.

Scene II—The Talbo house. That evening.

ACT ONE

ACT ONE

SCENE I

A Sunday afternoon late in September.

We see: the Talbo house—that is, a painted, extremely stylized curtain representing its dull-tinted exterior. It is a two-story house with four top-floor windows. On the ground floor there is a stoop and front door (the door is real; it must work). Accounting for the remainder of the lower floor is a dining room. This dining room is, as it were, a picture framed by the curtain—it is embedded there, like the scenes inside of sugar Easter eggs.

At the back of the dining room there are two moderately large windows hung with pink and gold-tasseled draperies. Through these windows can be seen the reddening, yellowing lonely limb of a tree. At the right, in the rear, is the kitchen door, a swinging door which is open, revealing an impressionistic glimpse of the kitchen: linoleum, the pan-littered black end of an old-style stove.

A pink rose-patterned paper covers the walls of the room. Many pictures, daguerrotype portraits, paintings of oversized fruit and flowers, vegetables, of fowls and huge fish, are hung in peculiar positions—as though the purpose had been to obscure various stains. At the left, along the wall, there is a mahogany sideboard; spindly glass cabinets, three at least, are filled with crystal and china, gewgaws. There is a tall rubber plant in one corner, a profusion of fragile chairs. A cuckoo clock decorates the wall above the sideboard.

The focus of the room, the dining table, one capable of seating six, is situated in the center of the stage. Suspended

3

above it there is a crystal and ruby-glass chandelier. A fish bowl inhabited by a solitary and enormous goldfish occupies a prominent part of the table.

Seated at the table is: COLLIN TALBO—*a sturdy, well-made, yet rather homely-faced boy of about fifteen. He is wearing a white shirt with rolled-up sleeves and a pair of khaki summer trousers, and he is smoking a cigarette. Sitting catty-cornered beside him is* CATHERINE CREEK. *She is a colored woman, chunky and rough-voiced. She appears to be dressed for a party. She is wearing a fancy calico dress; in one hand she clutches a handkerchief. A turquoise necklace is strung around her neck, her ears are studded with turquoise earrings, six of her fingers are stuffed with rings. She is working a jigsaw puzzle which is spread on the table before her.*

CATHERINE

It's a good thing you got your growth, because now you'd stunt it for sure; smoking and dancing and floozies—those are among the several things that will stunt a boy's growth and drive him crazy.

COLLIN

I don't know any floozies.

CATHERINE

(Frowning worriedly at the goldfish bowl)

Buster's eyes look right swollen: always staring—what does he find to look at so much? (*Then to* COLLIN) You don't know anything *but* floozies. (*She fits a piece of the jigsaw puzzle*) Except for Dollyheart; and naturally myself. There is no such thing as an Indian floozy.

COLLIN

Exactly now—which side of your family were Indians?

CATHERINE

All sides. I've told you so one hundred and fifty thousand times. Why don't you stop lolling around and spend your energies in a profitable manner?

COLLIN

(*Stubbing out his cigarette on the sole of his shoe and dropping the butt into the cuff of his trousers*)
Yeah? Why don't you?

CATHERINE

(*Indignantly*)
Who feeds you, Collin Talbo? Washes and irons and darns your clothes? and totes your slopjar?

COLLIN

(*Rocking back in his chair so that it is balanced on its rear legs*)
Dolly.

CATHERINE

(*With a crestfallen shrug*)
Well—Dolly and me, it's the same thing. It's just that I've got to be particular: things catch me here—(*She grabs the small of her back*)—and here. (*She thumps her chest and coughs*) But what I say is, why don't you get a hammer and nails and build a chicken coop? Or learn the French language?

COLLIN

(*Bored*)
Uh huh. Why don't you? Instead of wasting your life on a jigsaw puzzle?

CATHERINE

I *know* the French language. You recall that winter three winters ago Dolly and me improved us-selves? *Je suis fatiguée* —that's all I need to know. But a man and ladies are different.

COLLIN

No foolin'. What did you do—read that in the paper?

CATHERINE
(*Thoughtfully*)

A man should be a scholar and brood about business. A lady like Verena, like That One, she is not a lady. Mind you, I'm the first to give That One credit—if you sit down and think about it we nearly own this town; and every bit of it is That One's doing. (*She shakes her head, heaves a disgruntled sigh*) But you surely can't say the earning of it, all the property and all, you can't say it's made her an easy woman: (*Mimicking*) Who left the water running in the bathroom? Which one of you broke my umbrella? Dolly, you get rid of that kitten, you want to aggravate my asthma? . . . (*She breaks off exasperatedly*) And like today—hollering at us to kill all the chickens and plow up the vegetable garden, all on account of this little Dr. Morris Ritz is coming for Sunday supper . . .

(*During* CATHERINE'S *speech,* COLLIN *has risen and walked to the windows where he stands, his back to the audience, gently tapping his fingertips against the glass.*)

COLLIN
(*Remaining at the window*)
But just who is he? Old Dr. Morris Ritz?

CATHERINE

You haven't seen him slinking along the street like a lizard? Only what he's a doctor of and what his credentials are, that is a mystery. (*She fits a puzzle piece*) This I do know: him and That One are up to something in the business line. I can smell it. She met him in Chicago last July when she was there on that buying trip—then suddenly three days ago he pops up here in town living at the Lola Hotel. Twenty-five years we've lived in this house and That One has asked maybe exactly two gentlemen to take a meal here. So naturally I was considerable surprised when she says this morning fry up all the chickens and shell all the peas and dust all the china and iron all the linen and—lordamercy!—(*She wipes her forehead with her handkerchief*) on account of Dr. Morris Ritz is coming to Sunday supper. I said Miss Verena, well, I said, I'm innerested to know now who is this funny-looking little Dr. Morris Ritz. And That One says, getting all white around the mouth, well sir, he's not so funny-looking as *some* I could name. . . .

(*Unnoticed by* COLLIN *or* CATHERINE, DOLLY TALBO *has, during the last third of the preceding speech, appeared in the kitchen doorway; then, as* COLLIN *laughs at* CATHERINE'S *concluding lines, she comes into the room with a swift fragile-footed quietness; her presence is a delicate happening. She is a small pretty woman. Her movements are quick and yet uncertain; it disturbs her to make the most ordinary decision—whether to place a saucer here, a fork there. She is wearing a white, virginal, almost ankle-length dress and a somewhat frayed pink apron. She is carrying an elaborate bowl of roses.*)

7

DOLLY

Hush now, hush. (*She waves, not knowing where to put the roses*) Hush now. Poking fun at Verena. (*She deposits the roses on the sideboard*) Supposing she heard you? I will not tolerate having anyone hurt her feelings. She works very hard to provide the comforts you enjoy—that we all enjoy. In her own home she should have a sense of peace and affection.

CATHERINE

I'm affectionate. I have an affectionate nature. But Dolly-heart, dear child, you are not blind to the fact that That One has a cold place in herself concerning myself. About today— she says Catherine I spec you better wear a nice uniform for when Dr. Ritz comes to dinner. Now Dollyheart, you know it's not that I exactly object to being mistook for common kitchen help—besides which That One has never laid out to buy me uniforms. Here's what she said, said: Trot over and borrow one off Mrs. Gilbert's Ginger Jones. To humiliate *my*self before Ginger Jones!

DOLLY

(*Counting silver and collecting table linen from the drawers of the sideboard*)
Hush now. Hush.

CATHERINE

. . . as if me and Ginger Jones wore the same fit. You could wrap up this table in a pair of her step-ins. She must weigh . . . Collin, sugar, what would say is Ginger Jones's weight?

COLLIN

(*Absent-mindedly, and still gazing out the window*)
How much she weighs? Something like the same as you.

CATHERINE
(*Grimly*)

That's inneresting. That's an inneresting piece of observing. I see you forget that you are obliged to me for the mere circumstances of having grown to ordinary human size. If it wasn't for my treatments you'd still be a little runt like Biddy Skinner—and folks tell how he's had offers from the circus. But I took pity; oh yes, I pulled at your legs and tugged at your head until inside of two years I'd stretched you from four foot nine to five foot seven. . . .

COLLIN

Jesus, Catherine, you ask me how much somebody weighs. For Christ's sake . . .

DOLLY
(*With her hands over her ears*)

Please. This is Sunday: it's so important to toe the line. And Collin—while I remember—Verena is upset that you didn't go to church this morning. I told her that you had a pain. So do try to look as though you were in some sort of agony. (COLLIN *staggers with cross-eyed abandon away from the windows and leans on the table*) Not drunk, dear: in agony. (*Suddenly, from the sideboard drawers where she is selecting linen and silver, she lifts a paper sack*) Fancy this— my bag of jellybeans; really, I'd looked everywhere. (*She nibbles at one, then drops it back in the sack*) They do seem a bit moldy. Catherine . . . you've always wanted to get some colored pebbles for Buster's bowl. And these are just like pebbles—(*She advances upon the goldfish bowl*) and such lovely colors . .

9

CATHERINE
(*Clamping a protective hand over the bowl*)
Hold off! Buster here, he'd go for those jellies like a shark. It's not like he was young; you got to watch his diet.

DOLLY
(*As though reminded*)
Diet . . . I had a letter from Mr. Culver Joy.

(*Searching in the dress pockets under her apron, she produces a pair of partially shattered spectacles and several envelopes.*)

CATHERINE
Mr. Culver Joy from Joy City? That's one of our best customers.

DOLLY
This is from his granddaughter. Says: (*She adjusts the glasses and reads*) "Dear Miss Dolly Talbo. We appreciate all the grand work your dropsy cure medicine did for our granddaddy but we will not be needing any more bottles as Bless His Soul he passed away night before last. He would eat pork and that's what did it." (*Looking up*) I *told* them not to feed that man any pork. Specifically I said no pork or greasy foods. And not any sugar. . . .

CATHERINE
(*Piously*)
There's no blame can be attached to us, Dollyheart. We did our best. He was tempted. (*Then with genuine melancholy*) But gracious knows it's a big loss; he's been a standing order three years, Mr. Culver Joy.

DOLLY

Now there's somebody new. For instance . . . (*She unfolds another letter*) here's a Mrs. Clyde W. Dwyer; she lives in Arrow Springs. . . .

COLLIN
(*Reading over her shoulder*)

"Dear Miss Talbo, I have the dropsy something terrible and have tried many remedies that have lessened my complaint not one whit. Word has reached me that you brew a homemade dropsy cure that beats all. Kindly send me a trial bottle. It surely will do me good if my husband doesn't get at it first: he is a devil drunkard who will drink anything." . . .

DOLLY
(*Eagerly*)

Where does it say that—that last part? (COLLIN *laughs, and* DOLLY *seeing it is a joke, playfully swats at him. She puts the letters back in her pocket*) But that makes eight new orders: we'll have to make two trips to the woods this week. . . . I want to get enough herbs to carry us through the winter. Why—do look at that. . . . (*She means the cuckoo clock above the sideboard*) Collin honey, look in the kitchen and call me the time. Says twelve . . . I wonder, did it stop at midnight or at noon?

(*She drags her chair over to the sideboard. As* COLLIN *exits into the kitchen,* DOLLY *climbs on the chair to fiddle with the clock.*)

COLLIN
(*Offstage*)

Half-past four.

THE GRASS HARP

CATHERINE
(*Calling to Collin*)
I'll skin you if you gobble them chicken livers. You know
Dollyheart won't touch nothing but them chicken livers.

COLLIN
(*Entering, he lifts* DOLLY *off the chair, whirls and
swings her to the floor, singing:*)
Roses are red, violets are blue, sugar is sweet, and so are
you.

DOLLY
(*Anxiously freeing herself from Collin's arms*)
But four-thirty! And the table's not even set! . . . Clear
away that jigsaw. . . . (*Grabbing a tablecloth from the sideboard and shaking it out*) . . . And Collin, go brush your
teeth, put some shine on your shoes. . . .

CATHERINE
(*Calmly thwarting Dolly's attempts to arrange the
tablecloth*)
Hold off. . . . I've been working at this jigsaw going on
nine days. There's only maybe two dozen pieces left. Give
me a hand, Dollyheart, let's see what the picture is.

COLLIN
It's a windmill—and tulips—and those wooden shoes . . .
(VERENA TALBO *enters. The illusion must be that
she is passing on a sidewalk in front of the house. She
is dressed in black and grey. She wears gloves and
carries above her a black parasol. Her hat is black
straw decorated with a grey dove. She has tucked
under her arm a small paper-wrapped parcel. A small*

12

woman giving an impression of height, she walks as though she were part of a slow and haughty procession; her posture is severe, her manner exalted. She crosses the length of the stage and, folding her umbrella, disappears through the front door into the house. During this entrance, the scene in the dining room has continued; which is to say, there has been no interruption of dialogue.)

DOLLY
(Holding a handful of puzzle pieces)
Here's an eye. Blue. Anyone there with a missing blue eye?

CATHERINE
Honey, there's whole *heads* missing.

DOLLY
(She looks at the clock; at just this moment VERENA *is entering the front door)*
. . . We won't have any heads either if Sister . . . This belongs there.

(She tries to jam into place a piece of the puzzle.)

CATHERINE
(Wrenching it out)
No it don't. It's the wrong shape entirely. Look for a little wiggly piece.

DOLLY
(Sorting the pieces)
Wiggly? *(The door of the dining room opens—it is* VERENA, *who enters still wearing her hat and carrying the*

paper parcel. The others do not immediately look at her; they tense with an awareness of her presence; then COLLIN *moves again toward the windows, as if to escape the range of her gaze*) (*Smoothing her hands on her apron and turning to face* VERENA) Sister—we didn't expect—is our guest here? Everything—(*She glances at the clock*)—everything is ready —almost . . .

VERENA
(*Advancing to the table and putting her parcel there, then slowly pulling out the long pins that fasten her hat*)

Yes. Yes. Your efforts are evident. (*A sarcastic pause; she takes off her hat and jabs the pins into the brim*) Get that nonsense off my table.

(*She sweeps the jigsaw puzzle onto the floor; not with fury—rather, a serene, casual impatience.* DOLLY *hesitates an instant; presently she stoops and begins gathering up the puzzle, dropping its pieces into the fold of her apron.* COLLIN *helps her; but* CATHERINE, *sitting with an averted head, works her lips in a ceaseless soundless cursing.*)

DOLLY
(*As she is picking up the puzzle*)

Everything *is* ready, Verena. We were just about to set the table. Do peek in the kitchen—there's going to be fried chicken and ham. English peas. Rolls. *Banana* pudding. (*Her voice ascends with enthusiasm*) Two kinds of cake and tuttifrutti ice cream from the drugstore.

VERENA
(*Ignoring* DOLLY)

I've brought you a uniform. (*She slides the parcel on the*

table toward CATHERINE) You will go to your room and scrape the paint off your face. You will bathe. . . . I cannot have you smelling like a sow in the spring. You will clean under your fingernails and remove the jewelry: this is a private home, not a café.

CATHERINE
(*She does not and never will look at* VERENA *directly*)
I'm no kin to you. I'm no kin to you.

DOLLY
(*Rising from the floor where she has finished collecting the puzzle*)
Hush. Hush now.

CATHERINE
Hush. Hush. (*She gets up from her chair and picks up the goldfish bowl, holding it in the crook of one arm*) It's not me you're telling to hush; it's you, Dollyheart, it's yourself. Hush.

(*She slaps her hand against her heart; she moves toward the kitchen door repeating "hush, hush," and each time striking her heart.*)

VERENA
(*Imperturbably removing her gloves*)
The uniform.

DOLLY
(*Taking the parcel from the table and carrying it to Catherine*)
Please . . .

(CATHERINE *accepts the parcel and exits into the kitchen. Simultaneously* COLLIN *is more or less sneak-*

ing toward the dining-room door which has been open since Verena's entrance. But VERENA *has eyes in the back of her head—she "sees" him.)*

VERENA
Collin—were you excused?

COLLIN
(From the door's threshold)
Yes, ma'am.

VERENA
Yes, ma'am?

COLLIN
Yes, ma'am, I wasn't excused.

VERENA
You were not in church?

COLLIN
(Exchanging an apprehensive glance with DOLLY*)*
I had gee an awful toothache.

VERENA
(Turning to give him an appraising look)
Then it shall be taken out. I will call Dr. Skinner this evening.

COLLIN
Well, it wasn't altogether my *tooth*—stomach gripes . . .

VERENA
I shouldn't wonder—at your age, the drinking you do. All those roadhouses on the highway: I've a mind to have the

proprietors jailed. But Collin, my dear, it is simply later than you know. I won't always be able to stand between you— and the penitentiary.

DOLLY
(*She has been distractedly setting the table*)
Oh Verena! Sister!

VERENA
But one thing is certain. Maude Riordan's papa has denounced to me your conduct with his daughter. Is it true you shine flashlights in her window at night? And throw pebbles? And tempt her into the yard?

COLLIN
I have a right to. She's my girl friend.

VERENA
That will stop.

COLLIN
My particular girl friend.

VERENA
(*Her hand twitching in a gesture of disgust and dismissal*)
Take these with you and leave them in the hall on the hat-tree. (*She means her hat and gloves, which are lying on a chair beside the table; he comes forward to collect them*) And Collin, at least today behave as though you were a gentleman. . . . I know how difficult that will be considering certain inheritances—but—I value Dr. Ritz's esteem.

COLLIN

Yes, ma'am.

(*He exits through the dining room door.* VERENA *seats herself facing the audience; though she closes her eyes and folds her hands, her posture is rigid and her knees primly together. The light at the windows and in the room has deepened, is bluer, and* DOLLY, *who previously has set two candlesticks on the table, now lights them.*)

DOLLY

I wish you wouldn't scold him so—nor say what you do about "inheritance." He knows you mean his father. . . .

VERENA

(*With her eyes closed and her voice distant*)

He should be reminded.

DOLLY

How reminded, Sister? That they're dead: his mother Mary, our cousin Mary, such a pretty pretty pretty girl . . .

VERENA

He killed her—with his trips and his drinking and his women . . .

DOLLY

She loved him. Mary would not have loved anyone really wicked.

VERENA

Hateful man. Hateful.

DOLLY

(*Going to the sideboard for the bowl of roses*)
But he's dead . . .

VERENA

Most opportunely—he owed me eleven hundred and
forty-three dollars.

DOLLY

(*Placing the roses between the burning candles in
the center of the table*)
I was against Collin coming here—it seemed wrong, raising
a boy in a houseful of women. I feel differently now: maybe
because I'm selfish and wouldn't like the sound of this house
within Collin in it. Anyway I don't worry: I know he'll get
on, he'll make his mark. Because he's smart, so much smarter
than Catherine or me . . .

VERENA

That of course is claiming a great deal. Smart. As I remember, he was in the fifth grade two years—and now they
won't even allow him *in* the schoolhouse!

DOLLY

And good. You're so taken up, oh you've never seen him,
Sister—when he would come from the outdoors in the cold
weather and his cheeks like this—(*She cups a rose in her
hand*)—and fill himself with a bushel of biscuits. And when
we go to the woods to hunt our herbs he knows where the
pennyroyal is, and the best sweetmary. A boy who knows
such things is good, Verena; he'll get on. . . .

19

VERENA
(*Wearily*)

Do be still a moment.

DOLLY
(*Coming behind Verena and gently resting her fingertips on Verena's temples*)

You *are* tired, Sister. It worries me every night when I wake and see the light still burning under your door. And I wonder, Verena—why not close your ledgers, sell the stores. We could have long mornings drinking coffee in the kitchen.

VERENA

Oh Dolly, that's what I promised Papa—promised him to protect you, make it possible for you to sit long mornings in the kitchen with your puzzles and your jokes. Sit in the kitchen: that's for women and children. (*With a wistful longing*) I wouldn't know how. (*Suddenly staring at the table, then standing up*) Why have you set only two places?

DOLLY
(*With her head lowered and mumbling*)

I thought we—Collin and myself—we would eat in the kitchen with Catherine.

VERENA
(*She goes to the sideboard and returns bringing additional plates and silver with which she proceeds to reset the table*)

Don't fool with me, Dolly; don't tax me. This is important. Dr. Ritz is coming here expressly to meet you.

DOLLY

To meet *me*?

VERENA

What is more, I'd appreciate it if you'd hold up your head: it makes me dizzy, hanging like that.

(DR. MORRIS RITZ *enters in the same manner as* VERENA *did—walking, as it were, on a sidewalk in front of the house. A skinny, dagger-faced man with a slick small mustache, his clothes have the checkered gaudiness of a race tout's, and he walks with a jazzy cockiness, all the while snapping his fingers and whistling "Yessir, She's My Baby.")*

DOLLY
(*Deeply disturbed*)
But—he will *look* at me. I couldn't, I can't . . .

(*A bell rings: it is* DR. RITZ, *who reaches the front door. At the sound of it* DOLLY, *looking terrified, skitters around the table, as if hunting a corner to hide;* VERENA *tries to halt her, but she escapes and rushes out swinging closed the kitchen door. Meanwhile, the front door is opened for* DR. RITZ *by* COLLIN. COLLIN *has put on a jacket and tie.)*

DR. RITZ
(*Laughing: his laughter is like a nervous disorder*)
Ha ha—uh—ladies of the house at home? Ritz is the name.

(COLLIN *steps aside silently for* DR. RITZ, *then closes the door. In an instant we see them enter the dining room where* VERENA, *falsely composed and smiling, advances to shake his hand.)*

21

VERENA

Ah, Morris—so good of you. Have you met Collin? Collin is my poor cousin Mary's boy. He lives with us.

(DR. RITZ *laughs and slaps* COLLIN *on the back; at the same time his eyes are shrewdly swerving about the room.*)

DR. RITZ

Real old family mansion you got hold of here, Verena. Pretty ritzy. Ritz: ritzy. Ha ha.

VERENA

My sister is so anxious to meet you. (*Calling toward the kitchen door*) Dolly—Dolly, dear. (*After a pause, she calls more sternly*) I say, Dolly!

CATHERINE
(*Poking her head out the kitchen door*)
Dolly's flat on her back. Her bowels is bad.

(*She withdraws.*)

DR. RITZ
(*Nervously*)

Ha ha. Ha ha.

VERENA
(*To* COLLIN, *motioning toward the kitchen door*)
Collin.

(COLLIN *exits into the kitchen.*)

DR. RITZ
(*To* VERENA, *not whispering, but in a subdued, somewhat conspiratorial manner*)
Well, my dear, have you—ah—broached the matter?

VERENA

(*Shakes her head, looks troubled, then*)

Not yet, I don't want her to think we're taking anything *away* from her. It is for her own ultimate good. . . . (*Shakes her head again*) . . . Such a fearful burden to be the only grownup in a houseful of children: they have no one to depend on except me—and I have no one except myself.

DR. RITZ

(*Taking* VERENA'S *hand*)

You can depend on me, Verena.

VERENA

Someone else told me that—once. (*Looking at* DR. RITZ) I believe you. If I didn't . . .

DR. RITZ

But we must get the recipe. I've had answers from three firms in Chicago ready to place orders on the basis of the samples we sent them.

VERENA

(*Harassed, excited, almost whispering*)

All right. All right. I will, Morris—now, today . . . (*On the words "I will, Morris," the kitchen door opens and* COLLIN, *with a coaxing gesture, brings* DOLLY *into the room.* VERENA *takes* DOLLY'S *hand and pulls her forward to meet* DR. RITZ, *smiling*) Dolly dear, this is our guest—Dr. Morris Ritz from Chicago.

DR. RITZ

(*Offering his hand*)

A rare pleasure, to be sure . . .

(DOLLY *shyly gives her hand to* DR. RITZ, *who receives and kisses it noisily.*)

23

VERENA

Morris, will you sit here next to Collin. (*The seating arrangement at the table is as follows:* DR. RITZ *and* COLLIN *side by side,* DOLLY *and* VERENA *at either end of the table*) I hope you don't expect more than plain home food—very plain, I'm afraid.

(*She rings a small silver dinner bell.*)

DOLLY
(*As though suddenly wakened*)
Oh but it's a *lovely* dinner today, Sister. (*She looks at Dr. Ritz*) With tuttifrutti from the drugstore and two kinds of cake, and banana pudding.

DR. RITZ
(*With a sickly expression*)
No sweets for me. (CATHERINE *enters with a platter of fried chicken. Although she has not removed her jewelry, she is wearing the uniform* VERENA *brought her—it is blue and fits her like a sausage skin; the skirt is hiked well above her knees. She serves* DOLLY *first, then offers the platter to* DR. RITZ. *Examining the chicken dubiously,* DR. RITZ *continues:*) Tell you the truth, the only piece of chicken I can digest is the liver. Don't suppose you'd have that back in the kitchen, mammy?

CATHERINE
(*Menacingly*)
Dollyheart's done took them livers on her plate.

DOLLY
(*Embarrassed*)
But let me pass them to you. . . .

24

VERENA

She wants only sweet things anyway. You've noticed that the whole house smells of vanilla extract? Of course that's partly because Dolly wears it as a cologne.

DR. RITZ
(*Changing plates with* DOLLY)
If you're sure you don't mind ... (*He sneezes explosively*) Those roses—old allergy—kachoo!

DOLLY
(*Seizing the roses and carrying them to the sideboard*)
I am sorry—it never struck me you could catch anything from roses.

CATHERINE
(*Exiting into the kitchen*)
You can't.

COLLIN
(*Gnawing a chicken leg and addressing* DR. RITZ)
Excuse me. I'm interested. Do you cut people open?

DR. RITZ
(*Whimpering*)
Cut people?

(CATHERINE *enters with two vegetable bowls; hereafter she will move back and forth between the kitchen and the dining room carelessly overloading the table with various dishes.*)

VERENA

How nasty, Collin. Morris isn't that kind of a doctor—he's a pharmacist.

> (DOLLY *has clicked the wall switch that lights the chandelier; she is at the windows drawing the gold-tasseled draperies against the deep dusk.*)

DR. RITZ

I'm what you could—uh—call a chemical engineer.

DOLLY
(*Turning from the windows*)

You make medicines? We make a medicine, Collin and Catherine and me. We have customers all over the state.

DR. RITZ

Why sure, Miss Dolly—that dropsy cure of yours is a famous product.

> (*He and* VERENA *exchange a meaningful glance.*)

DOLLY
(*Disbelieving*)

Truly? You've heard of it?

DR. RITZ

Would *I* kid you? (CATHERINE, *returning to the kitchen, pauses in the doorway—she stands there alertly listening*) But tell me now, Miss Dolly—between you and me—what kind of stuff are you putting in this dropsy cure? (*Glancing again at* VERENA) It sorta, you might say, defies the analyzing methods of modern science.

DOLLY
(*Flattered but coy*)
A little of this, and well, a pinch of that ...

CATHERINE
(*Proudly*)
That's Dollyheart's own secret. Don't nobody know, not
me or Collin or nobody, we don't know all of it that goes
into the dropsy.

DOLLY
(*Shyly*)
It *is* a secret. I—I learned it from the gypsies.

VERENA
(*With forced sweetness*)
Dear, do tell Morris that old story of yours—about the
gypsies.

DOLLY
(*She is standing; she rests her hands on the back of
the chair in which she has previously been sitting and
begins the story in a manner that is at first self-conscious, then gradually less so; she loses herself, her
voice widens*)
Once—once when we were children—Verena with her
babyteeth and Catherine no higher than a fence-post—there
were gypsies thick as birds in a blackberry patch: not like
now, when maybe you see a few straggling through each
year. They came with spring: sudden, like the dogwood pink,
there they were—up and down the road and in the woods
around. But our men hated the sight of them. Papa said he
would shoot any he caught on our place. And so I never told
when I saw the gypsies taking water from the creek or steal-

ing old winter pecans off the ground. (*She hesitates; she clasps her hands together*) Then one evening, it was April and raining, I went out to the cowshed where Fairybell had had a new little calf. And there in the cowshed were three gypsy women, two of them old and one of them young, and the young one was lying na—(*She stutters, she glances at* DR. RITZ *with embarrassment*)—naked and twisting on the cornshucks . . .

VERENA

Not that. Not all that. I mean about the medicine.

DOLLY
(*So concentrated she has not noticed the interruption*)
. . . When they saw that I was not afraid, that I was not going to run and tell, one of the old women asked would I bring a light. So I went to the house for a candle, and when I came back the woman who had sent me was holding a red little hollering baby upside down by its feet, and the other woman was milking Fairybell. I helped them wash the baby in the warm milk and wrap it in a scarf. (*She sinks into her chair and, as though she were offering it to a fortune teller, holds out her palm*) Then one of the old women took my hand and said: Now I going to give you a gift by teaching you a rhyme. It was a rhyme about evergreen bark, dragonfly fern—and all the other things that Collin and Catherine help me find in the woods: (*She chants*) Boil till dark and pure if you want a dropsy cure! (*As though coming out of a trance, she looks at the others around the table; her voice grows self-conscious again*) In the morning they were gone, the gypsies. I looked for them in the fields and on the road. There was nothing left of them but the rhyme in my head.

DR. RITZ
(*Dreamily*)

Gypsy Queen Dropsy Cure—it's a natural! (*He clears his throat*) But Miss Dolly, how do you go about making it, what's your process?

CATHERINE

That's Dollyheart's secret.

VERENA

Very well, Catherine. Kindly close the door. (*Without moving from where she is,* CATHERINE *reaches out and shuts the door*) With yourself behind it.

(CATHERINE *exits into the kitchen; presently she opens the door a crack and we see her listening.*)

DR. RITZ
(*To* DOLLY)

You were saying . . . ?

DOLLY
(*Slicing for herself a piece of cake*)

Well—most every Saturday we go to the woods. Those are the River Woods down past the field of Indian grass. We have a tree-house. (*She picks crumbs off the cake and pecks at them like a bird*) Collin will tell you about the tree-house; he built it. . . .

COLLIN
(*With an ashamed shrug*)

It's a tree-house. . . .

DOLLY

(*Carried away*)

Oh but a *beautiful* tree-house—like a raft floating in the leaves: so cool in the summer, and now in the fall, when you can hear the wind through the Indian grass and with the colors so fine—I really could live there! (DR. RITZ *titters nervously; fingering his bow tie, he gives* VERENA *a strained, inquiring glance.* VERENA, *in a mood of mounting impatience, purses her lips, drums her fingers on the table*) We have picnics in the tree; then we hunt for herbs. The *secret* ones, the ones that make a *difference*, I find those myself. (*Proudly*) We get a dollar a bottle, divided between us three ways . . .

VERENA

(*Bunching her napkin and throwing it on the table*)

Stop. Just stop. (DOLLY, *startled, lets fall back onto the plate a batch of cake crumbs.* COLLIN, *too, stares at* VERENA; *and* CATHERINE, *opening the kitchen door wider, leans halfway into the room. Breathing deeply and recovering to a degree of composure,* VERENA *continues*) Without any further deviation, list for Morris the ingredients of . . .

DR. RITZ

(*Fervently, as though he already sees this trademark on a thousand billboards*)

The Gypsy Queen Dropsy Cure!

VERENA

That is what we want to know.

DOLLY

(*Bewildered*)

I don't understand, Sister. You never cared about it before.

Except you always said there would be trouble if we poisoned somebody. (*She lowers her head, almost whispers*) Is it because you're afraid we'll poison somebody?

VERENA
(*Rising, she walks around the table, moving slowly and as though she is planning what she will say. She grips the back of Dolly's chair*)

Do you understand money? Many thousands of dollars? That is the extent to which I "care about" your medicine. You see, Morris and I have made—an arrangement. We've bought the old canning factory back of the depot. We plan to bottle the dropsy cure there.

DOLLY
(*Disbelieving*)

My—*not*—my . . . ?

VERENA
(*Spinning round to confront her*)

I won't be crossed, I warn you. (*Then more calmly*) This is no childish proposition: I've planned it for a long time. (*Again placing her hands on the back of Dolly's chair*) Morris and I are going to Washington this week to register a patent—naming you as the inventor, naturally. Of course we will need the complete formula. Morris, will you write this down . . . ?

(DR. RITZ *extracts from his inside suit pocket a pen and pad: he waits like an expectant stenographer.*)

CATHERINE
(*Stepping away from the door*)

Don't you do it, Dollyheart. That One and This One—

31

(*She points to* DR. RITZ) they're nothing but crooks out to steal our dropsy.

VERENA
(*She takes a seething, silent step toward* CATHERINE)
Get out. (*A second step*) Out. (*Another step*) Out. (CATHERINE *backs through the kitchen door. There is a pause.* VERENA *looks a long look at* DOLLY, *who is sitting as if she were in a coma*) We're waiting.

DOLLY
(*Quietly*)
It won't do. Because you haven't any right. You haven't any right, Verena. (*She rises; she looks at* DR. RITZ *with dignity*) Nor you, sir.

DR. RITZ
(*Putting away the pen and pad*)
Maybe—uh—ha ha—uh another day. (*He stands up*) Verena—uh—if you want me I'll be at the hotel.

VERENA
(*With her eyes set hypnotically on Dolly*)
Collin, take Dr. Ritz to the door. (COLLIN *sulkily obeys her; he and* DR. RITZ *exit through the dining room door. We see* DR. RITZ *come out the front door. He walks swiftly across the stage—midway he stops, snaps his fingers, lifts his eyebrows and exits into the right wings whistling "Yes Sir, She's My Baby." During this, the scene in the dining room has remained fixed, a tableau:* VERENA *staring at* DOLLY, DOLLY *looking at the floor. Then* VERENA *glides toward the table*) These are facts! (*She raps her knuckles on the table; she does this at the end of each of the following sentences, accom-*

panying these gestures by moving a step or two nearer DOLLY *who, in her turn, takes an awkward step backwards; thus they circle around the table, always several feet apart*) I paid three thousand for that old factory. Have four carpenters working out there at eighty cents an hour. Seven thousand dollars worth of machinery already ordered. Not to mention what a specialist like Morris Ritz is costing. And why? (*She lets the question echo, then*) All for you!

DOLLY
(*Sad and failing*)

All for me? (*Then earnestly*) You are my own flesh, and I love you tenderly; in my heart I love you. I could prove it now by giving you the only thing that has ever been mine: then you would have it all. Please, Sister—(*She falters*) let this one thing belong to me.

VERENA
(*Bitterly*)

You speak of *giving*. All these years that I've worked like a fieldhand: what haven't I given you? This house, that . . .

DOLLY

You've given everything to me. And to Catherine and to Collin. Except—we've earned our way a bit. We've kept a nice home for you, haven't we?

VERENA
(*She laughs and circles the table, glaring around her*)

Oh a fine home. You and that baboon. (*She motions toward the kitchen*) And that other little scoundrel. (*She stops to look at* DOLLY *directly*) Has it not struck you that I never ask anyone into this house? And for a very simple reason: I'm *ashamed* to.

DOLLY
(*As though the breath has gone out of her; she sinks into a chair*)
I'm sorry. I am truly. I'd always thought there was a place for us here, that you needed us somehow. But it's going to be all right now, Verena. We'll go away.

VERENA
(*Sighing*)
Poor Dolly. (*She picks up a spoon and snuffs the candles; the chandelier dims*) Poor poor thing. Wherever would you go?

DOLLY
(*After a moment's wait*)
I know a place.

(*Slow curtain*)

ACT ONE

Scene II

In the absolute darkness we immediately hear music—a long lyrical wail that, rising, runs away into a frivolous and chasing melody. The following characters wait on the blacked-out stage for a spotlight to take its turn in picking them out: the REVEREND'S WIFE *and the* REVEREND, *the* BARBER, *the* BAKER'S WIFE, *the* POSTMASTER, *the* SHERIFF. *Each of these people will be separately spotlighted for a scene of his own, the music bridging each appearance.*

The music fades as the spot falls first on: the REVEREND'S WIFE *and the* REVEREND.

REVEREND'S WIFE
(A bull-voiced woman whose steel-rimmed spectacles are too small for her vast and brutal face. She is carrying a market-bag and is dressed for the street— a thin black topcoat and a rather stark little hat. The REVEREND, *standing somewhat behind his wife, is a small man in a dour too-tight suit. His* WIFE *is, in effect, addressing a friend)*

Edna, you don't know, you don't know, my dear. The Reverend my husband and I were with her just now. A heart-rending sight—wasn't it, Reverend . . . ? *(She looks at her husband, who tries to get out a word of reply, but she booms on, shutting him up)* Utterly prostrated, she is. No, it's not every day that you find out your only sister is a *lun*atic. Of course *we* could have told her that lo these many years. Conceive of it—ransacking, looting Verena's things right and left and running off in the middle of the night! Not telling a soul. Oh Edna, what fearful heavy crosses the best of us have to tote. And Verena Talbo, she's among the best of us, we can't deny that. No, there's not a notion in the world where they've got to. (*With freezing intensity*) I wish I could lay hands on them . . .

(*Blackout. The music dances, then dies down as the spot picks up:*)

BARBER

(*A tiny mincing man, a chatterbox with a shrewd spinsterish voice. His greying hair is parted in the middle. He is wearing a barber's smock: in one hand he has a pair of scissors, in the other a comb: with these he makes a pantomime of giving a haircut*)

Say what you will, Mr. Grump—for myself I relish a little excitement. And really this is blissful—there hasn't been anything like it since Tubby Twotoes got locked in the ice plant and froze to death. Folks have been swarming in and out of here asking what do I know why Miss Dolly took off to Jesus knows where. I say: at the bottom of the barrel you'll find that fellow calls himself Dr. Ritz. Mr. Grump, you ought to thank your stars you're not in my trade—this Dr. Ritz was here for a trim and afterwards I *scalded* my hands trying to sterilize them: his scalp was that much of a scandal. So the way I figure it—him and Verena were up to some nefariousness that Miss Dolly found out about and even she couldn't stomach. I say good for her: nothing would tickle me more than to see Verena Talbo get her come-uppance. A little tonic, Mr. Grump?

(*Blackout. Music. The spot shifts to:*)

36

BAKER'S WIFE

(An ample woman with a good-natured manner, in short, a person anyone ought to like. She is wearing a sweater and a very long apron. Her hair looks as though she had mopped it around in a flour barrel; there is flour on her face and hands. She is speaking to an imaginary customer)

No, Mrs. Amory—there's not a fresh roll in the place. I burned them all up. I might as well close down the bakery— burned up everything all morning. I can't keep my mind on anything what with this worrisome news about Miss Dolly Talbo. It worries me sick to think about her and old Catherine running off from home and creating a scandal like they have. A bit peculiar they may be, Mrs. Amory, but they're as good women as you'll find. Only in a little town like this, prominent citizens have to behave themselves; if they don't, the whole place goes crazy. *(Sniffing) Sakes*, just smell it! There go all my gingerbreads!

(Blackout. Music. Spot to:)

POSTMASTER

As is the custom in many rural towns, this postmaster, an elderly dry-voiced fellow, doubles as the telegraph agent. He is coatless: his striped shirt has a starched, very high white collar. . . . He is wearing green sleeve-supporters and a green eyeshade; in his hand he holds a batch of telegrams. He has a habit of rocking from one foot to the other. He is talking, we presume to a friend)

Matter of fact, took in quite a haul this morning, Fred. Sent off fifty copies of a fifty-nine-word telegram. *(Poring through the sheaf of telegrams)* About Miss Dolly Talbo:

her—uh—disappearance. (*Finding the particular telegram*) Fred, don't say I said this, but it says: (*Reading*) "Be on the lookout for following persons believed traveling together. Dolly Augusta Talbo, white, aged fifty, light brown hair, not likely to be dangerous. Post description bakeries as she is cake eater. Catherine Creek, Negro, pretends to be Indian, age about fifty, strong, likely to be dangerous. Collin Talbo, age fifteen, bad posture, surly natured. All three wanted as runaways." (*Shuffling the telegrams together again*) With the fifty copies, that cost Verena Talbo over a hundred dollars. I don't doubt she's took to her bed.

(*Blackout. Music. Spot to:*)

SHERIFF

(*A youngish man, squat, powerful, a bully with a rabble-rousing voice. He is wearing a leather jumper to which there is pinned a silver Sheriff's star; He has on riding breeches and laced-up boots and sports a pistol in a hip-holster. He is haranguing what we must believe to be a large group of men*)

Boys—now boys, as sworn-in deputies, you-all raise your arms and swear to do your duty. (*Lifting his arm*) Say: I swear to do my duty. (*Offstage male voices echo him; he lowers his arm*) Your duty is—is to find these damn fools. We've got a warrant (*Slaps his pocket*) on grounds that they plundered and stole property belonging to Miss Verena. What I'm driving at is—is we ain't dealing with no ordinary missing persons. What we got is—is a case of *crime*. Now boys, they can't have got far: was only one train through here last night—and *it* didn't stop. (*Pointing with his thumb*) Brophy, Big Eddie, Sam, you there, you-all get your flash-

lights and have a look down all the old water-wells—you
never know where you might find fools like them!

(*Blackout. The music comes up fast, and with an
added weight, a more somber excitement achieved,
perhaps, by the steady roll of a small drum. The
music should weave through the following sequence
and never quite fade. Spot on:*)

REVEREND'S WIFE
(*Breathlessly speaking into a make-believe telephone*)
Hello, Edna—I was so afraid you weren't going to answer
because—listen. Edna, they've *found* them—well, not exactly
found them. But old Mr. Vanevery over at the graveyard, he
saw them around dawn this morning—he said they were
headed *into the woods!*

(*Spot to:*)

BARBER
(*Into telephone*)
.... *into the woods?* But *which* woods?

(*Spot to:*)

BAKER'S WIFE
(*Into telephone*)
River woods, you say?

(*Spot to:*)

POSTMASTER
(*Into telephone*)
All I've got to say is, they ain't found them yet. River
woods is a big place.

(*Spot to:*)

SHERIFF

(*With a broad gesture to the crowd*)

River woods, boys! Everybody together and into the woods!

(*Blackout. The music continues.*)

ACT ONE

Scene III

As the curtain slowly rises the music changes into a strange and shimmering song, a sound of grass and wind, leaves, voices. The scene is mid-morning in an autumn wood, and the stage is dominated by a luxurious tree with thick surface roots and a gnarled, very foreshortened trunk; on either side the branches extend almost the width of the stage—the effect should be more airy than dense; its leaves, rust and speckled, green and greenish gold, are shivering in a wind, rippling like the colors on a peacock's tail. In the lower center of this tree there is a tree-house, a sturdy raft that must suitably accommodate four persons; it is fully exposed to view and, because the trunk of the tree is in trick perspective, will seem rather higher up than actually it can be. At the left of the stage we see the beginning edge of a field of tall straw-blonde grass. A painted backdrop, looming behind the tree and curving into the flies, suggests sky and birds, the depths of a forest; at night it will shine with a sprinkling of stars. There are plants and falling vines of ivy; and at the front of the stage, at the right, there is a small moss-colored mound scattered over with leaves.

DOLLY and COLLIN are seated in the tree-house surrounded by a collection of cardboard boxes and cloth sacks. DOLLY is wearing a long-skirted suit of dark and durable material; around her shoulders there is a dainty sealskin tippet; and she is wearing a hat, a bonnet really, decorated with what was known in other days as a "traveling veil." She is in a listening attitude, her feet dangling over the edge of the tree-house.

41

COLLIN *is sitting at her left with his legs crossed Indian-fashion. He is wearing tan trousers, a blue sweater, a tan muffler.*

For some while after the curtain has gone up we hear the music, and it is as though its theme has set the scene in motion; the grass trembles, the leaves sway, paper butterflies, suspended by silk threads, swirl and flutter. Gradually the music is like a call that has almost ceased to echo. A certain stillness settles.

DOLLY

Do you hear? That is the grass harp.

COLLIN

(*With a searching glance*)

Where?

DOLLY

Oh not anywhere. The wind. There in the great field of grass. (*A whispery rush of music, then*) A harp of voices—telling a story. It knows the stories of everyone; and when we are dead it will tell ours, too.

COLLIN

If the story was about me . . . (*A pause, then*) What would it say?

DOLLY

It would say—it would say what you did when you lived. I've often heard my papa. When we were girls he used to stomp around on cold mornings and sing songs while he built the fires. I've heard the grass telling about those cold mornings.

(CATHERINE *enters. She is very dressed up in a navy-*

blue cloth coat and a black straw hat decorated with celluloid cherries. She is carrying the goldfish bowl.)

CATHERINE
(*Singing as she enters*)
"Sister Mary wore three lengths of chain
Ev'ry link was Jesus' name!
Oh, I ain't gonna grieve, gonna grieve my Lord
Ain't gonna grieve, gonna grieve my Lord
Ain't gonna grieve, gonna grieve my Lord, my Lord no more.
"Oh, the tallest tree in Paradise
Christians calls it the Tree of Life,
Oh, I ain't gonna grieve, gonna grieve my Lord
Ain't gonna grieve, gonna grieve my Lord.
Ain't gonna grieve, gonna grieve my Lord, my Lord no more."

COLLIN
(*To* CATHERINE)
Where was you so long?

CATHERINE
(*Holding the goldfish bowl up to the light and scrutinizing it*)
One thing I was doing, I was down to the river freshening the water in Buster's bowl. He can't breathe in no dirty water. Give me a hand, sugar, help us up. (*There are easy footholds in the tree-trunk and strong trailing vines to grip*) Gonna fall, gonna bust our heads—don't I know it!

COLLIN
I don't see why the hell you wanted to bring that fish with you anyway.

43

CATHERINE

(*Settling herself on top of a box that is between, and a little behind, Collin and Dolly. The fishbowl is held in her lap and she idly stirs the water with her finger*)

Least he don't sass me like some. Just now, down to the river, the current was so strong and Buster got swept right out of the bowl. He could have swam way away. All I did was whistle to him (*She whistles*) and he come straight back into her. (*She taps the bowl*) He don't leave me and I don't leave him. (*Suddenly to* DOLLY) What's ailing you, Dollyheart? You hearing dead folks again? (*A breeze rustles the leaves, the grass; we hear the whistlings of a whippoorwill, a mockingbird*) Every time this time of year you start hearing dead folks. But sugar, that's only the grass has gone dry now and the wind makes it sound funny.

DOLLY

But the wind is us. (*Leaning her head on Catherine's knee*) It gathers and remembers all our voices, then sends them talking and telling through the leaves and the fields. . . . I've heard Papa clear as day.

CATHERINE

All I wish, I wish a powerful big breeze would blow all that foolishness out of your head and set you so studying our predicament. We are homeless people with few assets. Exactly now, what are our assets?

(DOLLY *extracts a man's wallet from her pocket and makes a muttering count of dollars and small silver.*)

44

COLLIN

Biddy Skinner owes me five bucks—maybe I should walk into town and get it from him.

CATHERINE

Uh uh. You'd just take that money and scoot off to the poolhall. Besides which, we can't none of us separate.

DOLLY
(*Completing her tabulations*)
. . . twenty-five and ten makes thirty-five. We've got forty-three dollars and thirty-five cents. And my cameo.

CATHERINE

I know somebody rode a bus the whole way to Mexico City, Mexico—for fifteen dollars.

DOLLY

That's nice, dear. But we can't go to Mexico. We don't speak the language. And it's a very dry sort of place. No rivers and forests; and without a forest, how could we make the dropsy cure? I think we ought to stay right here.

COLLIN
(*Reluctantly, and as he lights a cigarette*)
But we can't.

CATHERINE

You recall how we saw in the paper where a man bought a castle across the ocean and brought it every bit home with him? If he could do that—what's to keep us from loading some rooms of our house on a wagon and hauling them down here?

45

DOLLY

Nothing. Except that it's *not* our house. It belongs to Verena.

CATHERINE

You wrong, sugar. If you feed a man, and wash his clothes, and born his children, you and that man are married, that man is yours. If you sweep a house, and tend its fires and fill its stove, and there is love in you all the years you are doing this, then you and that house are married, that house is yours. The way I see it, the house up there belongs to *us:* in the eyes of God, we could put That One right out.

DOLLY

Yes, but . . .

COLLIN

(*Rising and leaning his hand against an upper branch*)

Maybe I'll go over to Pensacola and join the navy. I could join the navy and send you my paycheck.

CATHERINE

(*Scornfully*)

I'll bet you'd send it, too.

COLLIN

Sure I would. You'd be my dependents.

DOLLY

No, no. Always wondering where you were—I would feel so old.

46

CATHERINE

Not that I'm against you contributing to our support—
with a steady honest job.

COLLIN
(*Peevishly*)

I'm hungry.

CATHERINE

Well, there's plenty to eat. (*She puts the fishbowl down
beside her, then starts rummaging in a box*) We won't starve
a while yet. I stripped the pantry—didn't leave a biscuit for
That One's breakfast.

(*She begins passing food out of the box, apples,
oranges, cupcakes. Suddenly, like a cracking whip,
we hear a distant-sounding rifle-shot. Silence, a lonely
crying of birds: the occupants of the tree-house sit
galvanized—as one their heads turn and they gaze
expectantly at someone the audience cannot yet see.
It is* JUDGE CHARLIE COOL *who, staring up into the
foliage and the sky, enters walking backwards. He is
carrying a rifle; a batch of dead squirrels, attached
to his trouser belt, swings against his hip. The trousers
are faded khaki, he is wearing a sharkskin wind-
breaker, army shoes, and an old yellowed corduroy
hunting cap. He is a retired county circuit judge of
sixty, youthful-looking and with a modest and coun-
trified manner. As he approaches, the three in the
tree seem to hold their breath:* DOLLY *lowers the veiling of her hat, as if to camouflage herself;* COLLIN
squats on his haunches; CATHERINE, *with her hands
over her face, peeks between spread fingers. The*
JUDGE *reaches the far right front of the stage and*

pauses; he aims his gun, pointing it toward the audience, then gradually he swings the barrel around until his aim is within inches of the tree-house.)

CATHERINE

Judge Charlie Cool! Don't you dare shoot us!

DOLLY

(Timidly)

Please—I'd be obliged if you wouldn't.

JUDGE

(Lowering his rifle and letting out a startled hearty laugh that ends on a puzzled note)

Well, good day. Good day, Catherine Creek, Collin boy. *(Lifting off his cap)* Is that you, Miss Dolly?

DOLLY

(With dignity)

It is.

JUDGE

What happened—a wildcat chase you?

CATHERINE

Wildcats! Where you see any wildcats?

DOLLY

The Judge is only spoofing. *(Doubtfully)* Aren't you?

JUDGE

No ma'am. I've tracked several big cats in these very woods. Course they won't be bothering you—they don't come out till night. (CATHERINE *and* DOLLY *exchange a serious glance*) But Miss Dolly, say now, what *are* you folks doing up there?

DOLLY
(*After a thoughtful moment*)
Sitting.

JUDGE
I can see that, but uh . . .

DOLLY
(*As though to change the subject*)
A fine mess of squirrels you've got there, Judge.

JUDGE
(*Detaching the squirrels from his belt*)
Take a couple. They're real tender if you fry them in deep fat. (*Leaning his gun against the tree-trunk*) Wait a minute, I'll bring them up to you.

DOLLY
(*Alarmed*)
You needn't do that. Just leave them on the ground.

JUDGE
(*Hoisting himself up into the tree*)
Better not. Ants will get at them.

(*Everyone shifts to make more room for the* JUDGE; *and* COLLIN, *climbing a little higher into the tree, straddles a branch above their heads and sits there eating an apple.*)

49

JUDGE

(*Pounding his foot on the boards*)
A tree-house. And a dagderned good one.

CATHERINE

Won't be if you don't quit that stomping.

DOLLY

Won't you sit down, Judge, and join us in a small repast?

JUDGE

I can't say I mind as I do. That's kind of you. My daughter-in-law, she doesn't set much of a table—she doesn't believe in breakfast at all. (*Seating himself*) Not like my wife: Irene came from hardy stock, she understood a man ought to eat—long as she lived I never went without an adequate breakfast: pork chops and mashed potatoes and squirrels and possum . . .

DOLLY

(SHE *and* CATHERINE *have been exploring the food packages together*)
May I offer you a drumstick?

JUDGE

Thank you, ma'am. (*After biting into the drumstick, and as he chews*) Reason I didn't know it was you a while ago, Miss Dolly—I couldn't see you for all that veil.

DOLLY

(*Raising and pinning back the veil*)
I believe it's customary for ladies to wear a veil when they go traveling. We intend to travel—eventually.

JUDGE

Don't.

DOLLY

What—wear a veil?

JUDGE

Travel.

DOLLY

Oh it's not that we *want* to. None of us are travelers—we've never been anywhere. Except once on Collin's birthday we went to Birmingham and saw the Ringling Brothers, Barnum and Bailey. I enjoyed the freaks very much.

CATHERINE

One of them freaks, Judge, you bear a resemblance to him. In the face. The rest of him was all feathers. He went quack quack quack.

COLLIN

It was a fake.

CATHERINE

Was not!

COLLIN

Was so.

CATHERINE

You said every one of them was a fake—cause you were jealous. Jealous of them freaks cause they were so unusual and the center of attention. (*Staring at the* JUDGE) . . . A striking resemblance.

DOLLY
(*Nibbling a cupcake*)
Anyway—that's the only time we ever went anywhere.

JUDGE
You have a good home, all of you. Stay in it.

DOLLY
(*Despairingly*)
Yes.

CATHERINE
Tell the Judge the truth. How That One and the little rat
was stealing the dropsy ...

DOLLY
Hush. Now hush. I mean it.

JUDGE
(*With soft-spoken concern*)
Are you in trouble, Miss Dolly?

CATHERINE
Trouble! Don't let me *commence!*

DOLLY
(*To Catherine, icily*)
Have you no particle of pride?

CATHERINE
Who are you? My Dollyheart or some kind of hypocrite?
The Judge, he's a friend, he ought to know how after a life-
time of toil we were shown the door of our own house.

DOLLY

For one thing, we weren't shown the door. We left. (*With lowered eyes*) I can't bear talk against my sister. She's worked hard, she deserves to have things as she wants them. It's our fault, someway we failed her. . . . (*Shuddering, beginning to cry gently*) . . . There was no place for us in her house.

JUDGE

Don't weep. Don't weep, Miss Dolly.

CATHERINE

(*Using the lifted hem of her skirt to dry Dolly's eyes*)

All them tears—they'll stain our pretty clothes. . . .

JUDGE

It may be there is no place for any of us. Except we know there is, somewhere; and if we found it, but lived there only a moment, we could count ourselves blessed. This could be your place. (*Looking up into the tree*) And mine.

CATHERINE

(*As she finishes drying Dolly's eyes*)

You can have my share. You surely can. Judge, please sir, lend me one of them cigarettes.

DOLLY

(*In a voice still choked and tearful*)

Catherine! I've never known you to touch tobacco.

CATHERINE

It must be a comfort, so many folks speak in its favor;

and Dollyheart, when you get to be our age you've got to look for comforts.

(*She puffs amateurishly at a cigarette the* JUDGE *has lighted for her.*)

DOLLY
(*Intensely curious*)
What is it like?

CATHERINE
Delicious. Want a taste?

COLLIN
(*Suddenly alert and listening*)
Shh! Shh!

(*The leaves rustle, there is a perceptible darkening of light. The rolling of a small drum signals the entrance and accompanies the actions of the following characters. Those entering from the right are: the* REVEREND, *the* REVEREND'S WIFE, *the* CHOIR MISTRESS, *and a rolypoly man called* BIG EDDIE STOVER. *Those entering from the left are: the* SHERIFF, *accompanied by two men, one called* BROPHY, *the other* SAM. *They do not come in as a group, but, stalked by the drumbeat, appear separately or in stealthy pairs. The* REVEREND *is a scrawny man, smaller than his wife, and he is wearing a black suit and a black fedora. His* WIFE *and the* CHOIR MISTRESS, *a thin severe woman with an odd baby-talk voice contradictory to her appearance, cautiously walk hand in hand. It is the* CHOIR MISTRESS *who first sees the congregation in the tree. She nudges the* REVEREND'S WIFE—*the drum stops with dramatic abruptness as these ladies stare raptly up at the tree-house. Then, in unison, they take a step backwards and scream.*)

SHERIFF
(*With his hand on his hip-holster*)
All right now, come down from there, the lot of you!

REVEREND'S WIFE
(*To the* SHERIFF)
We agreed to let the Reverend tend to this—in the merciful manner of the Lord's name. (*The* JUDGE *laughs; she gives him a withering look*) You've lost your mind, have you, Charlie Cool? What are you doing with these people in the first place?

JUDGE
(*Rocking as though he were in a rocking chair*)
Just a-sittin' and a-talkin'. Any objection?

REVEREND'S WIFE
Shame! For shame!

CHOIR MISTRESS
(*Baby-lisping*)
Shame. For shame!

REVEREND
(*With an air of getting in a word edgewise*)
I speak to you on behalf of your sister, that gracious good woman . . .

REVEREND'S WIFE *and* CHOIR MISTRESS
(*Together*)

That she is!

REVEREND

. . . who has this day received a lamentable shock.

REVEREND'S WIFE *and* CHOIR MISTRESS
(*Together*)

That she has!

REVEREND

How can you have come so far from God as to sit up in a tree like a drunken Indian?

CATHERINE
(*Flat-voiced*)

I resent that.

DOLLY
(*Casually dusting her skirt*)

Consider a moment, Reverend, and you will realize that we are nearer God than you—by several yards.

JUDGE
(*Chuckling appreciatively*)

Good for you, Miss Dolly. I call that a good answer.

REVEREND'S WIFE

I'd thought you were a Christian, Judge Cool. My ideas of a Christian do not include laughing at and encouraging a poor mad woman.

JUDGE

Mind who you name as mad, dear lady. That isn't especially Christian either.

REVEREND'S WIFE
(*Defensively*)

It's a fact—she is—she's a lunatic.

CATHERINE

Hold on. Hold on, preacher lady. One more word, I'll come down there and slap you bowlegged.

REVEREND'S WIFE
(*Turning to the others, gasping, stunned*)

Every one of you: you're witnesses. You heard what she said, that black—black . . .

(CATHERINE, *pushing back her sleeves, starts to get up.* DOLLY *and the* JUDGE *restrain her.*)

REVEREND

Answer me this, Charlie Cool. We are here to do the Lord's will. . . .

CHOIR MISTRESS
(*Lisping*)

In a spirit of mercy.

REVEREND

. . . Are you a disbeliever in the Lord's will?

JUDGE
(*Amused*)

The Lord's will? You don't know what that is any more

than I do. For myself, I think the Lord must be very satisfied to see us sheltered in one of his trees.

SHERIFF
(*Advancing, and ready for action*)
To hell with all that!

REVEREND'S WIFE
(*To the* SHERIFF)
Under no circumstances will we tolerate swearing. Will we, Reverend?

SHERIFF
(*Turning on the* REVEREND)
I'm in charge here. This is a matter for the law.

JUDGE
(*Quietly*)
Whose law, Sheriff? Remember that I sat in the court-house twenty-four years. Take care. You have no legal right whatever to interfere with Miss Dolly.

SHERIFF
(*In coaxing, wheedling tones*)
Miss Dolly, you've always been a peaceable person. Come down. . . . (*With a foothold in the tree-trunk and extending his hand as if to help* DOLLY) . . . Come home: you don't want to miss your dinner.

DOLLY
We've eaten, thank you. Have you? There's another drum-stick if you'd like it.

SHERIFF
(*Climbing determinedly toward her*)
You make it hard on me, ma'am.

JUDGE
All right, Sheriff. You lay a hand on any one of us . . .
(*He raises his foot*) I'll kick you in the head.

> (*The* SHERIFF *keeps climbing toward the tree-house.
> and the* JUDGE *kicks at him—whereupon, amid much
> hollering, the following things happen: The* SHERIFF
> *catches the Judge's foot and starts to pull. The man
> called* BIG EDDIE STOVER *pulls at the* SHERIFF, *and
> the other two men,* BROPHY *and* SAM, *join this tug-
> of-war chain—with the* REVEREND *struggling at the
> end.* CATHERINE *holds onto the* JUDGE *and prevents
> his being pulled out of the tree-house; then* COLLIN,
> *coming down from his higher perch, takes over this
> job, and* CATHERINE *fetches her fishbowl; with a
> hand carefully applied to the rim to keep the fish
> from spilling out, she begins to pour the water onto
> the Sheriff's head. Throughout this* DOLLY *has sat
> with a squeezed up face and with her fingers in her
> ears. Then suddenly the* JUDGE'S *shoe comes off in
> the Sheriff's hand: the* SHERIFF, *his three* DEPUTIES
> *and the* REVEREND *all crash back on one another and
> collapse on the ground. The* REVEREND'S WIFE *and
> the* CHOIR MISTRESS, *augmenting the disaster, kneel
> beside the fallen men with whining cries of distress.*)

REVEREND'S WIFE
(*Trying to lift her husband*)
Speak to me! Speak! Are you dead, lover?

(COLLIN *and the* JUDGE *descend from the tree-house.*
THE JUDGE *stands and hops on one foot so that his
shoeless foot does not touch the ground.*)

JUDGE
(*To the* SHERIFF, *who is picking himself up*)
I'll thank you for my shoe.

SHERIFF
(*Viciously throwing the shoe at the* JUDGE)
If you weren't so old, I'd damn well knock you down.

JUDGE
(*As he stoops to put on the shoe*)
I'm not so old, SHERIFF: just old enough to think men
ought not to settle their differences in front of ladies.
(*Straightening up and clenching his fists*) On the other hand,
I'm ready if you are.

SHERIFF
(*After spitting between forked fingers*)
Hell, I'm not going to take the blame for hitting an old
guy.

JUDGE
Or the credit for standing up to one either. Go on, tuck
your shirt in your pants and trot along home.

SHERIFF
(*Appealing to Dolly and Catherine in the tree*)
Save yourself a lot of trouble: get out of there and come
along with me now.

(*Neither* CATHERINE *nor* DOLLY *stirs, although*
DOLLY *drops her veil, as though lowering a curtain
on the subject once and for all.*)

REVEREND'S WIFE
(*Portentously*)
Never mind, Sheriff. They've had their chance. (*She starts
to exit, the* SHERIFF, *her husband and the others following
after her. The same drum-rolls that accompanied their entrance attends their departure, and the lighting darkens to a
richer, deeper color. Then, just before she goes offstage, the
REVEREND'S WIFE turns round and the drum halts*) You
may think you are getting away with something. But let me
tell you there will be a retribution—not in heaven, right
smack here on earth!

CHOIR MISTRESS
Right smack here on earth!

(*The drum returns, continues until the last of the in-
truders has exited. Then, as the set dims to a silvery
twilight, music falls, and a transitional time lapse, in
the most stylized sense, occurs before our eyes.* DOLLY
and CATHERINE *climb down out of the tree,* CATH-
ERINE *carrying a bundle of two scrap-quilts.* SHE
*spreads the quilts on the ground over the exposed
roots of the tree. We see the* JUDGE *and* COLLIN
*gathering sticks and twigs for a fire which they build
(without "lighting" it) in front of where the quilts
have been spread. The music fades, like a last sigh of
wind—for a moment the silence sings with twilight
sounds, the shrilling of cicadas, bleating of frogs, the
mournful wail of whippoorwills.*)

61

DOLLY

(*Standing by the tree-trunk and a little leaning against it*)

You were very brave, Judge.

JUDGE

(*Adding sticks to the fire*)

No. I was afraid. I'm always afraid of righteous people....

DOLLY

However that may be, you are a brave man. (*As if to herself*) All of them behaving ugly that way, acting mad enough to kill us. Though I can't see why, or what it has to do with Verena: she knew we were going away to leave her in peace. I told her. (*Gazing around at the insect-sounding twilight*) But it's getting dark—you should be starting home.

JUDGE

Two women and a boy? With night coming on? And the Sheriff, those fools up to God knows what? I'm sticking with you.

(*He strikes a match and "lights" the fire: the shadows and colors of flame rotate.*)

CATHERINE

(*She is sitting on one of the quilts; she spreads her hands in front of the fire*)

That feels mighty good—only what we need is a sip of blackberry wine. Collin sugar, hop up there.... (*She means for him to go to the tree-house and bring down the wine*) I brought along two bottles case anybody was feeling the cold. I'm feeling it.

(COLLIN *climbs up into the tree.*)

Taken for *Life* by Photographer Cecil Beaton

DOLLY
(*Coming to the fire and holding her hands over it*)
But won't they be worried, Judge? Your family, I mean.

JUDGE
(*Soberly*)
They won't be missing me. We're not—close that way.
(*Breaking in half some sticks and piling them on the fire*)
I'm more like a roomer. They let me have my room.

> (COLLIN *has arrived with the wine and four tin cups.*)

CATHERINE
(*Passing a cup full of wine to each person*)
Dollyheart's daddy, old Mr. Talbo, every time he poured
hisself a little taste of something, he'd say: Here's winking
at the devil. Well . . .

> (*She raises her cup and the others follow suit.*)

COLLIN, CATHERINE, JUDGE
(*Together*)
Here's winking at the . . .

DOLLY
(*Strained and listening*)
Hush. Hush.

COLLIN
(*Looking off*)
It's only an owl. A snowy owl.

DOLLY

I keep imagining ... (*With a certain exhaustion she sinks to the quilts*) Do you think they will bother us again?

JUDGE

(*Nodding, and then*)

We must be ready for them. But if we are to defend our position, we must know what it is. We are in trouble—because we are troubled. (*Rolling a cigarette*) Miss Dolly, how long? Thirty, forty years? It was that far ago that I remember you—riding to town in your father's wagon—never getting down from the wagon because you didn't want us town children to see you had no shoes.

CATHERINE

(*Nudging* COLLIN)

What did I tell you? Not a shoe to our name.

JUDGE

(*Continuing to* DOLLY)

All the years that I've seen you, never known you, not ever recognized what you are: a spirit, a pagan ...

DOLLY

(*Mildly alarmed*)

A pagan?

JUDGE

Well—a spirit, someone not to be calculated by the eye alone. Spirits are the accepters of life; they grant its differences, and consequently are usually on the right side. Myself, I should never have been a judge; as such, I was too often on the wrong side: the law doesn't admit differences. Do you remember old Carper—the fisherman who had a houseboat down on the river? He was chased out of town—wanted to marry that pretty little colored girl, I think she works for Mrs. Postum now. And you know she loved him; I used to see them when I was fishing, they were very happy together. She was to him what no one has been to me: *the one person in the world*—from whom nothing is held back. Still, if he had succeeded in marrying her, it would have been the Sheriff's duty to arrest and my duty to sentence him. I sometimes imagine that many whom I've called guilty have passed the real guilt on to me: It's partly that that makes me want once before I die to be right on the right side.

CATHERINE

You on the right side now—if that's all it takes to satisfy you.

DOLLY
(*In a voice that lingers inquiringly*)
The one person in the world ..

JUDGE

I mean a person to whom everything can be said. Am I an idiot to want such a thing? But oh, the energy we spend hiding from one another, afraid as we are of being identified. But for us there is no longer any need to worry about the picture we present. . . . (*Gesturing toward the tree-house*) Here we are: four fools with a roost in a tree. The only problem now . . . (*He laughs*) . . . is to find out who we truly are.

CATHERINE

I know who I am.

JUDGE

By scraps and bits I've in the past surrendered myself to strangers—men who got off at the next station: put together maybe they would have made the one person in the world. But there he is with a dozen different faces moving down a hundred separate streets. This is my chance to find that man—you are him Miss Dolly, Collin, all of you.

CATHERINE
(*To the* JUDGE)

I should have told you—go easy on the wine: it's uh, *strong.*

DOLLY
(*To* CATHERINE)

Please—if you can't be respectful, then take a nap.

CATHERINE

I'm only saying: I'm no man with a dozen faces. The notion.

DOLLY

But Judge, I'm not sure I know what it is you have in mind we should tell each other. Secrets?

JUDGE

Secrets, no, no. Speak of the twilight, the fact there are no fireflies. What one says hardly matters—only the trust with which it is said, the sympathy with which it is received. (*Lighting his cigarette*) My wife, a remarkable woman, we might have shared anything, and yet, yet . . . (*Bringing the tips of his fingers together as if in illustration*) . . . We could not *touch.* She died in my arms, and at the last I said: Are you happy, Irene? Have I made you happy? Happy, happy,

happy, those were her last words: equivocal. I have never understood whether she was saying yes, or merely answering with an echo; I should know if I'd ever known her. My— son. He does not admire me. I've wanted him to, more as a man than as a father. Unfortunately, he and his wife feel they know something shameful about me.

DOLLY

You mustn't tell us if it pains you.

JUDGE

No—I'll tell you what it is: what it is they hold against me. Five years ago, nearer six, I sat down in a train seat where some child had left a child's magazine. I saw on the back cover addresses of children who wanted to correspond with other children. There was a little girl in Alaska. I sent her a picture postcard: Lord, it seemed a harmless and pleasant thing to do. She wrote me back—about her father's sheep ranch and the Northern lights. And she sent a picture of herself—a wise and kind-looking child. So I found an old Kodak made of myself on a fishing trip when I was fifteen— out in the sun and with a trout in my hand. I wrote her as though I were still that boy, told her of the gun I'd got for Christmas, how the dog had had pups and what we'd named them. To be growing up again and have a sweetheart in Alaska—well, it was fun for an old man sitting alone listening to the noise of a clock. Two years ago, when I told her I was getting ready for law school, she sent me a gold nugget. . . . (*He takes the nugget out of his pocket and holds it out for the others to see*) . . . It would bring me good fortune, she said.

DOLLY

And that's what they think is shameful? Because you've helped keep company a lonely little child in Alaska? It snows there so much.

JUDGE

(*Returning the nugget to his pocket*)

My son's wife, she found out about the letters. They think it all a sign of . . .

(*He taps his head.*)

CATHERINE

(*Extending her wine cup for* COLLIN *to refill*)

I had a letter once. Still got it somewhere. Kept it twenty years wondering who wrote it. Said Hello Catherine, come on to Birmingham and marry with me, love Bill.

DOLLY

A *grown* man asked you to marry him—and you never told one word of it to me?

CATHERINE

(*Shrugging*)

Well, Dollyheart, what was the Judge saying? You don't tell anybody everything. Besides, I've known a peck of Bills —wouldn't study marrying any of them. (*Thoughtfully*) What worries my mind is, which one of the Bills was it wrote that letter. It could be the Bill that put the roof on the chicken house; course, by the time the roof was up—my goodness, I have got old, been a long day since I've given it two thoughts. There was Bill that came to plow the garden one spring. That man sure could plow a *straight* row—went away on a Pullman job; might have been him wrote me that letter. Or Bill—uh uh, his name was Fred. (*Smacking her lips*) This wine is mighty good.

(*All four stare into the fire; we hear rustlings in the leaves, the hooting of an owl.*)

COLLIN
(*Frowning*)

I—you're wrong, Judge.

JUDGE

How so, son?

COLLIN

I'm not in trouble: I'm nothing—or would you call that my trouble? They kicked me out of school on account of I was such a troublemaker and couldn't even learn the alphabet; anyway, I never would have got past third grade if I hadn't caught Miss Burkett necking old Tubby Twotoes. So I lie awake thinking what do I know how to do: fool around. And I get scared when I think maybe that's all it will ever come to: fooling around. Another thing is, I'm *mean*. You probably heard the thing I did to Whitey Kuzak: grabbed hold of him and bit off a good hunk of his ear. . . . I said the reason was he insulted me: but pure meanness was why I did it. What I'm saying is, I've got no feelings—except for Dolly and I guess Catherine, which is different. I know a lot of girls; I even like one of them a whole lot.

CATHERINE

Floozies, that's all he knows.

COLLIN

(*To* CATHERINE)

Maude Riordan's not one ounce of a floozy, you hear me? (*To the Judge*) It's me—you'd be surprised—the thoughts in my head. Only with Maude I try not to have these thoughts. The night of the Baptist Church dance I made her one of those flower knickknacks girls wear here—(*He jiggles his breast*)—made it myself with sweetpeas—and I took her to a roastbeef and mashed-potato dinner at the Philadelphia Café. See, I wanted to be nice and decent—but then, after the dance I'm walking her home—and it's like somebody was running after us, this other me, the one with the thoughts. And I start running too—cause I don't want him to catch up with me: I just left Maude standing there in the road and ran like hell. You said before about the one person in the world. Why can't I think of her like that? . . . then I couldn't have just the thoughts about her that I have about other girls. Maybe, if I could care for somebody that way, I'd make plans and carry them out.

JUDGE

(*Turning up his collar*)

Son, I'd say you were going at it the wrong way first. (*Picking up a leaf off the ground*) How could you care about one girl? (*Twitching the leaf between his fingers*) Have you ever cared about one leaf? (COLLIN *catches up a leaf in his hand and stares at it. Mildly pressing the leaf against his cheek the* JUDGE *continues*) We are speaking of love. A leaf, a handful of seed—begin with these, learn a little what it is to love. First, a leaf, a fall of rain, then someone to receive what a leaf has taught you, what a fall of rain has ripened. No easy process, understand; it could take a lifetime, it has mine, and still I've never mastered it. . . . I only know how true it is: that love is a chain of love, as nature is a chain of life.

DOLLY
(*With an intake of breath*)

Then—I've been in love all my life. (*More lamely*) Well, no. (*Rising, she takes some steps away from the group*) No, I guess not. I've never loved a—a gentleman. You might say I've never had the opportunity. (*Moving, drifting as in a dream toward the moss-covered mound*) But—I have loved everything else. Like the color pink. When I was a child I had one colored crayon, and it was pink: I drew pink cats, pink trees . . . And the box I kept, it's somewhere in the attic now, I must ask Verena please to give it to me, it would be nice to see my first loves again. It's only—it's only a dried honeycomb, an empty hornet's nest, other things, oh an orange stuck with cloves and a jaybird's egg. (*Looking at the* JUDGE) Love *is* a chain of love. Because—when you love one thing, then you can love another, and that is owning, that is something to live with.

CATHERINE

I've got Buster up there. . . . (*She gestures toward the tree-house*) Just cause I like him don't make me love the world. Love a lot of mess, my foot. You can talk what you want— I say people ought to keep more things to themselves. The deep down ownself part of you, that's the good part: what's left of a human being that goes around speaking his privates? (*Lifting one of the quilts and wrapping it around her shoulders*) Judge, take this other quilt and wrap it round you. . . . (*To* DOLLY, *who is standing looking at the sky*) . . . Man's shivering like was Halloween.

71

(*Rising, the* JUDGE *takes the quilt and walks slowly toward* DOLLY, *who takes no notice of his coming but continues to stare up into the sky. He drapes the quilt over her shoulders.*)

CATHERINE
(*Drawing* COLLIN *under the wing of her arm*)
Snuggle up, hard-head: you cold like anybody else.

(COLLIN *and* CATHERINE *settle down, as if to go to sleep. The stage now is night-like, moon-lighted—the whippoorwills' call is clearer, longer.*)

DOLLY
(*Still gazing at the sky*)
What did you wish?

JUDGE
(*Standing behind* DOLLY)
Wish, Miss Dolly?

DOLLY
Didn't you see? (*Pointing*) There was a shooting star. (*Excitedly, and with her voice trailing as though she were following the shooting path of the star*) Oh . . . Oh . . . Look . . . Again! I hope you made a wish that time.

JUDGE
Yes . . . I did.

DOLLY
(*Looking at him over her shoulder*)
Tell me.

72

JUDGE

You first.

DOLLY

(*Looking back at the sky*)
I only wished—that I could see another one. And you?

JUDGE

My wish—Miss Dolly—won't you . . . ?

(*He glances round at* CATHERINE *and* COLLIN *to satisfy himself that they are asleep.*)

DOLLY

What . . . ?

JUDGE

(*Touching* DOLLY'*s shoulders*)
Be—the one person in the world.

DOLLY

(*Turning and facing him for a surprised moment; then, in a small voice*)
Could I be?

JUDGE

(*Smiling*)
I think so. But I would want you to decide.

DOLLY

It's what I would like, a life made of my own decisions.
Except I've never earned the privilege of making up my own
mind.

(*On the words "my own mind" the* JUDGE *bends forward, as if to kiss her; but quickly, in a rather*) *frightened way, she drops her hat veiling over her face. Gently, then, the* JUDGE *takes the rim of the veil and, as in a stately ceremony, draws it back. They look at one another. Music, tenuous, a thread, rises as the* JUDGE *leans and kisses* DOLLY'S *forehead. Slowly a scrim falls, we see them dimly behind it, and then, as the music climbs, there is projected onto the scrim a night sky streaked with a cascade of shooting stars.)*

(*Curtain*)

ACT TWO

ACT TWO

SCENE I

It is early morning of the following day, a time when day-break mists have still not dispersed. The scene is silent with sleep.

CATHERINE *and* COLLIN *are huddled asleep by the darkened fire. . . .* DOLLY, *the* JUDGE, *these two are in the tree-house; they are still upright wrapped together in a quilt and they are asleep with the* JUDGE's *head resting on* DOLLY's *shoulder.* DOLLY's *hat is rather askew and the* JUDGE's *hair is tangled on his forehead.*

Standing at the edge of the grass, really in fact posing there, we see MAUDE RIORDAN, *a girl of sixteen, slight, wistful, very pretty. She is carrying schoolbooks held together by a strap. On tiptoe, moving quickly and with the quality of a dancer, she approaches the burned-out fire and hovers an undecided moment above the sleeping* COLLIN.

MAUDE
(*Whispering*)
Collin . . . Collin. (*She touches him, and then, as though afraid of having done this, retreats several steps.* COLLIN *raises himself, opens his eyes and looks straight ahead, not seeing* MAUDE. CATHERINE *grumbles in her sleep, but does not wake up.* MAUDE *whispers:*) Collin . . . here I am.

(*Then* COLLIN *sees her, gazes at her as if she were part of some continuing dream. From a sitting position he falls forward on his knees.*)

77

COLLIN

(*Not whispering, but in a hushed voice*)
Aw, Maude. Aw, honey.

(CATHERINE *startles them with a rasping snore.* COL-
LIN *stands up; he and* MAUDE *steal softly to the right
of the stage.* COLLIN *reaches and pinches her arm.*)

MAUDE

(*Pained and rubbing the place he has pinched*)
You pinch so hard!

COLLIN

I thought I was dreaming because . . . Where did you
come from?

MAUDE

(*Pointing*)
From there—from the road and through the grass. I was
on my way to school—and then I wasn't. I heard you were
in the woods.

COLLIN

(*Grinning*)
I'll bet you heard.

MAUDE

(*Moving toward the moss-covered mound*)
There are terrible stories going around. Everybody at
everybody else's house. (*As she sits down*) Oh Collin, why
did you do it?

COLLIN

I didn't do anything.

MAUDE

You did. At least—they're going to put you in jail. All of you. I heard Daddy say so.

COLLIN

He'd like that, wouldn't he?

MAUDE

Well, I wouldn't. I wouldn't like it if they locked you in a jail maybe for years and years. (*With sudden dismay*) You'd even miss the party! Elizabeth Henderson and I are planning the most wonderful Halloween party—(*Sorrowfully*) real wine punch and everything.

COLLIN

A *party*. Good Jesus Christ!

MAUDE
(*Apologetically*)

But you do—think of little things like that. Even in the face of terrible disaster, you can think. Somebody I count on—somebody I love—won't be able to come to my party. You think of little things.

COLLIN

If you have a little mind.

MAUDE

That's not true. My grandfather was practically a genius. And when our house was burning down, what did he worry about? He worried because he heard the telephone ringing inside and there was nobody could answer it. (*A pause, then*)

79

Would you really have gone away—left town without saying a word to me?

COLLIN

Aw, honey, I was thinking of you. Fact is, I might join the navy.

MAUDE
(*Disappointedly*)

Oh.

COLLIN

You could be my dependent. *One* of them. I mean, I could send you the bus fare to come see me whenever my ship was in port.

MAUDE

I'm sure Daddy would never permit that. (*With a certain sly hopefulness*) Not unless we were—man and wife. (*There follows a strained silence.* COLLIN, *with a screwed-up face, scratches his head;* MAUDE *fiddles with the strap of her schoolbooks*) I guess I'd better go. I'm already late at school—you know what a fuss Miss Burkett will make. (COLLIN, *as though deep in thought, walks away from her. Rising,* MAUDE *looks wanly after him*) If I don't see you again . . .

COLLIN
(*Coming back to her; then, putting his hands in his pockets, and with a very simple air*)

It's going to be a nice day.

MAUDE
(*Looking round her*)

A lovely day—I think.

80

COLLIN

I know a shallow place where we could go wading back and forth across the river—the water's still warm enough. (*She shakes her head and without conviction*) This one day —for just a while: Maude, come with me.

MAUDE

I can't—don't—Daddy will find out I wasn't in school. . . .

COLLIN
(*Intensely*)

This one day.

(*Slowly* MAUDE *lets her schoolbooks slide to the ground and allows* COLLIN *to draw her forward by the hand. As they exit they pause once, glance apprehensively back at the sleepers and, as* MAUDE *laughs a hauntingly airy laughter, disappear with light-hearted lilting steps into the depths of the forest. At the sound of* MAUDE'S *laughter the lighting brightens to a more golden daylight and* CATHERINE *sits bolt upright. She does not see their exit, only hears the laughter, and stands up, turns around as though searching for its source.*)

CATHERINE
(*Yelling up into the tree*)

Dollyheart—that you laughing? Dollyheart—wake up there!

DOLLY
(*Opening her eyes and rubbing her temples*)

Don't scream—courtesy is so necessary: especially in the morning.

CATHERINE
(*Ominously*)

I heard laughing.

DOLLY

It must have been me; I had a very funny dream: that we'd all been turned into animals. . . . You were a walrus and Collin. . . . Where *is* Collin?

CATHERINE
(*Gazing round, then stamping the quilt as though he might be hiding in its folds*)

I knowed I was missing something. (*She walks to the left of the stage and calls*) Collin!

DOLLY
(*The* JUDGE *is still sleeping with his head on her shoulder; she taps his head with her knuckles as if it were a door*)

I hate to disturb you—excuse me—please, Judge, wake up. (*The* JUDGE *yawns, stretches himself, gives every indication of having come to life—then collapses again, sound asleep with his head nuzzling Dolly's shoulders. She shakes him severely*) No, no—you mustn't—do wake up.

(*The* JUDGE *gradually pulls himself together. While* DOLLY *has been rousing the* JUDGE, CATHERINE *has gone from the left of the stage to the right and, as in the first instance, calls:*)

CATHERINE

Collin! (*Then she wanders toward the front of the stage, her eyes hunting the ground as if for a clue to his whereabouts. She sees Maude's schoolbooks; she loosens the strap*

82

takes one out, and opens it, her eyes narrow, her teeth clenched) Maude Riordan.

DOLLY
(*To* CATHERINE)
What is it? (*She begins to descend from the tree, the* JUDGE *following after her*) What have you found?

CATHERINE
Maude Riordan (*Then handing the book to* DOLLY) There it is—her name, wrote down for all to see.

DOLLY
(*Taking the book and reading from the inside cover*)
Maude Riordan, eleven Cicada Lane . . .

CATHERINE
She done come here, sneaked here behind our backs and lured him with her wiles—though I don't know why a man would give her the time of day; so scrawny—nothing on her to pinch.

JUDGE
(*Teasing* CATHERINE)
Oh now—I wouldn't go as far as that.

CATHERINE
The floozy. Taking advantage of a boy's innocence to make him leave his loved ones. If they've eloped, I for one will never receive her.

JUDGE
(*In reply to* DOLLY, *who has turned to him with a distressed expression*)

It isn't that serious. I expect I know where they are. (*Again in reply to an expression of* DOLLY'S, *a questioning one*) After all, I've been Collin's age—and know the places in these woods where you might entertain a young lady.

CATHERINE

Then get out there and get them. Cut yourself a switch on the way.

JUDGE
(*After a few reluctant steps*)
Will you feel safe, Miss Dolly? I don't like it, leaving you alone.

CATHERINE

Nobody's alone. Dolly and us has always made out.

DOLLY

We'll have a pot of coffee ready for you when you come back.

JUDGE
(*Walking backwards toward the same exit we have seen* MAUDE *and* COLLIN *take*)
When I call like this . . . (*He yodels*) . . . you holler back: we'll keep in touch that way, and if I don't hear you I'll come running.

(CATHERINE *and* DOLLY *watch his exit.* DOLLY *continues to look in the direction in which he has gone, but* CATHERINE *takes a seat on the moss-covered mound.*)

CATHERINE
(*Resentfully*)
I saw you snuggling him. (DOLLY *looks at* CATHERINE

with a puzzled air) I wake up, first thing I witness: him smooched up to you like a little calf at his mama's titty.

DOLLY

(*With a light, yet embarrassed laugh*)
It was cold, we were cold. . . . Goodness, I never thought . . .

CATHERINE

Somebody was thinking—I don't say it was you. (DOLLY *sits down at* CATHERINE's *feet; she still has* MAUDE's *book in her hand*) Not proper; that's what it's not.

DOLLY

Oh it's proper. At least—Catherine dear, please don't *glare* at me—because if it's not going to make you unhappy, I want to tell you something. (*After a pause, during which she stares at the book*) Last night, the Judge—well, he proposed.

CATHERINE

(*She sits with an expression of perfect blankness for as long as it takes to count five; then, dead-faced*)
Proposed *what?*

DOLLY

(*At first surprised, then thoughtful*)
I'm not altogether sure—now that I think of it. It seemed to me he meant—of course he didn't really say it—marriage.

CATHERINE

(*She crosses her legs, as though it is a stunned reflex action, then breaks suddenly into a laughter that lasts until she has to wipe her eyes; gasping*)
Tell me—tell me every word what transpired.

DOLLY
(*Crossly*)

No, I won't. (*Ruffling through the pages of the book, vaguely pretending to read*) Not if you are going to laugh. I wouldn't anyway.

CATHERINE
(*She rises and, staring down at her, walks round to the other side of Dolly*)

Look at me—Dollyheart, is you sincere?

(*Offstage, from what must sound like rather a distance, we hear the* JUDGE's *yodel.*)

DOLLY
(*Anxiously*)

You'd better answer him.

CATHERINE
(*Folding her arms*)

Not me. I'm not speaking to him.

DOLLY

Please—he'll think something is wrong.

CATHERINE

Do it yourself. (*The* JUDGE *calls a second time, and* DOLLY, *standing up, attempts to answer him; it is a feeble, small sound*) (*With a gesture of exasperation she finally answers the* JUDGE *herself—indeed, blasts him in a voice strong enough to fell trees*) . . . Devil take him! I ought to have knowed, him and all that love-talk: *leaves*—love a leaf, my foot.

DOLLY

(*She has approached Catherine, and on the words "love a leaf" lays her hand on Catherine's wrist*)
You *are* angry. It isn't just put-on, is it?

CATHERINE

(*As though she has been touched, and in a gruff yet gentle tone*)
When you told me that—felt like you was going ahead of me, a different Dolly, all grown-up and different. And I couldn't follow you, I had to stay where I am: the same old me. (*A pause; then, with lowered eyes*) But Dollyheart, *would* you . . . ?

DOLLY

(*Moving a little away*)
He never really asked me. And if he had, I couldn't really answer. I guess I've never been required to make up my own mind: either you or Verena has always done that for me. But until I can—I will never know what is right.

(*At this moment we become aware of* MISS BABY LOVE DALLAS. *When we first see her she is mysteriously peering through a foliage of vine-leaves.*)

MISS BABY LOVE

(*First a shrill giggle, then*)
Anyone to home? (*Then she trips, so to say, into sight—a small creature full of bounce and strange good spirits. She is teetering on high heels and is dressed, on the whole, like a dance-hall hostess—there is a very dubious fur piece slung over her shoulder and she is carrying a red suitcase pasted with golden stars and pictures of Clara Bow, Jean Harlow, etc. Painted in silver lettering on either side of the suitcase is*

the legend "Sweetheart Cosmetics." Swinging this suitcase, she skips up to DOLLY *and* CATHERINE) I'm Miss Baby Love Dallas . . . (*As she puts down the suitcase*) . . . three times voted Sweetest of the Sweethearts traveling for Sweetheart Cosmetics. (*Squinting at* DOLLY) *You* can use everything I've got. (*Then looking at* CATHERINE, *too*) *Both* of you. If you'll just show me in the house . . .

DOLLY

There isn't any—real house.

MISS BABY LOVE
(*She snatches up her suitcase; then, with a hard and knowing look*)

What are you—hoboes? (*Glancing sharply around, then suddenly giggling*) Of course—it's a picnic! (*As she sails toward the moss-covered mound, there to deposit her suitcase*) Am I not a stupid wench? I didn't think you looked like hoboes. Only in my line of endeavor you can well imagine the escapes I've suffered: rape—and all that kind of thing. But oh the compensations are joyous—to bring beauty to the world. It's my duty: I park my little car on country roads and hunt through these backwoods for lonely houses where some poor hag is pining away for beauty. . . . (*She pops open her suitcase, and as she does so a music box starts to play, "Oh, You Beautiful Doll"*) Isn't that clever? (*She stretches her arms out to* DOLLY, *and, sort of dancing her way toward her, hums a tune. She takes* DOLLY *by the elbow and starts to push her toward the moss-mound—saying to* CATHERINE) Come stand over here and watch the miraculous change I'm going to wreck on Madam.

DOLLY

(*Protesting as* MISS BABY LOVE *forces her to sit down on the mound*)

Please—I beg your pardon—don't—I don't wear cosmetics —Miss uh Sweetheart.

MISS BABY LOVE

Miss Baby Love Dallas is the name. You have heard of the city of Dallas, Texas? It was founded by terribly close relatives of mine. (*The music box tune has run down.* MISS BABY LOVE, *grabbing a large rhinestone-studded mirror out of her suitcase, sternly thrusts it in front of Dolly's face; then, in a deep, threatening voice*) Look at yourself! (DOLLY *meekly does as she is told—then* MISS BABY LOVE *whirls round and holds the mirror up to* CATHERINE) You, too! (CATHERINE *lolls out her tongue, as though hunting evidence of illness.* MISS BABY LOVE, *with a shudder of disgust, promptly whips the mirror away; then, she looks into the mirror herself and with her little finger moistens and arches an eyebrow, saying as she does so*) But we mustn't give up hope. I can beautify anything. (*Humming "Oh, You Beautiful Doll" she pulls a perfume atomizer out of the suitcase and sprays it at them*) Scotland Fling—the odor of heather—direct from Paree, France—an exclusive with Sweetheart Products—fifty cents a pint. (*On the words "fifty cents a pint" we hear, off-stage, a familiar sound:* DR. RITZ—*whistling "Yessir, She's My Baby." He enters through the grass with a supremely confident strut. He is dressed as in Act One, and is wearing a straw hat. Delightedly eyeing* DR. RITZ'S *entrance,* MISS BABY LOVE *exclaims:*) Oh look yonder! . . . A *man.* (*She sprays him with her atomizer; he ducks*) Cute thing . . .

DR. RITZ

(*Acknowledging* CATHERINE *and* DOLLY, *who have received him with hostile silence; he tips his hat*)

Good morning, Mademoiselles. I can see the country air agrees with you. Wish I had time to store up some in the old . . . (*Striking his chest, and with a swift leer at* MISS BABY LOVE)—pardon the word—bosom. But the fact is . . . (*Glancing over his shoulder*) I'm in a bit of a dash.

CATHERINE
(*With a gesture*)

Dash on. Nobody here's keeping you. (*To* DOLLY) Want I should give the Judge a holler?

(DOLLY *starts to rise, as though to confront* DR. RITZ. *But* MISS BABY LOVE, *who has once again been rummaging in her suitcase, this time for a hairy powder puff and a handful of hair-curlers, forces her to sit down again.*)

MISS BABY LOVE

No you don't, dearie. Miss Baby Love has a little job to do on you. First, a nice powder base . . .

(*She lavishly dusts Dolly's face with the powder puff.*)

DR. RITZ

See, Miss Dolly, it's like this—I have a little proposition to make to you.

DOLLY

I don't believe, sir—that I care to hear it.

DR. RITZ

(*He laughs; then, producing a very fat envelope from his inside pocket, squats in front of Dolly*)

You don't have to listen—just use your eyes. (*He takes a thick sheaf of bills out of the envelope and begins to count them out in a little pile on the ground*) Fifteen hundred dollars.

MISS BABY LOVE

(*Arrested by the sight of Dr. Ritz's money, she eyes him with a greedy shrewdness*)

Tell me, dearie—haven't we met before?

DR. RITZ

Can't remember the pleasure. Dr. Morris Ritz, Chemical Engineer.

(*He takes her hand and kisses it noisily.*)

MISS BABY LOVE

(*With a gesture to herself*)

Miss Baby Love Dallas, Beautician (*Smacks her lips*) All the same I never forget a face—especially if it's my type.

DR. RITZ

(*Gives* MISS BABY LOVE *a sharply suspicious look; then, turning back to* DOLLY)

All right, Miss Dolly—(*Pointing to the money he has counted out*)—there it is. And mind you—this is merely a down payment. There's a firm in Chicago willing to pay a substantial amount for your dropsy recipe.

DOLLY

I have nothing to sell.

DR. RITZ
(*He picks up his money and rises; then, in an idealistic manner*)
What about the human race? Your dropsy cure, why it may be the very thing to remedy this old planet's ills. Have you right to keep that from your fellow human beings?

CATHERINE
Anybody wants our dropsy—all they got to do is send us a dollar's worth of money-order.

DOLLY
Did—did my sister send you on this errand?

DR. RITZ
That good lady, I'm afraid our set-up has been liquidated. I'm all for you—giving her the air. Why share our profits with her?
(*During the last six speeches* MISS BABY LOVE, *after pawing around in her suitcase, has produced a lurid-looking magazine. Having located a particular page, she has slunk around viewing* DR. RITZ *from all angles. On the words "giving her the air" she steps forward triumphantly brandishing the magazine.*)

MISS BABY LOVE
(*Rather slowly, and with a blackmailing quality*)
That's who you are. I told you I had a keen memory—so I'm remembering the latest issue of True Life Detective. It contains a very interesting picture—and information about a *reward*. (*With a wink*) Get me, dearie?
(CATHERINE *moves around to snatch the magazine away from* MISS BABY LOVE.)

92

DR. RITZ
(*Stuffing the money in his pocket; to* MISS BABY
LOVE, *sarcastically*)

Some little joker. A girl like you ought not to be on the
loose. What you need is a chaperone.

(*Off-stage, we hear two people calling; it is the*
BARBER *and the* BAKER'S WIFE.)

BARBER
(*Off-stage*)

Yoo-hoo . . . Yoo-hoo. Miss Dolly—where are you?

BAKER'S WIFE
(*Off-stage*)

Miss Dolly . . . Hello-o! Hello-o!

(*The* BARBER *and the* BAKER'S WIFE *enter through
the grass.*)

BARBER
(*Stopping dead at the sight of* DR. RITZ; *pointing*)

There he is—the crook; don't let him get away.

(DR. RITZ *starts directly toward the* BARBER *and the*
BAKER'S WIFE, *who cower before him. Then seeming
to change his mind, and with a tip of his hat, he
makes a hurried exit.*)

BARBER
(*Shouting after him*)

Stop thief! Stop!

93

MISS BABY LOVE
(As she picks up her suitcase; calling out in the direction that DR. RITZ *has exited)*
Wait for me, dearie—I'll give you a lift in my automobile.

(She exits after him.)

CATHERINE
(Bitterly slapping the magazine as she shows it to DOLLY)
He's wanted in six states. There was a thousand dollars reward for him. We done lost it.

BARBER
More than that, I'm afraid.

DOLLY
What do you mean, Mr. LeGrand?

BAKER'S WIFE
(To DOLLY, *gently)*
Miss Dolly, he stole Verena's money.

BARBER
All of it.

DOLLY
(Stricken; and as she stiffly sits down on one of the tree roots)
Oh.

BAKER'S WIFE
(Reprovingly)
Not all of it, Amos.

BARBER

Why quibble, my dear. At any rate all her cash: five thousand eight hundred dollars—so I'm told. (*The* JUDGE'S *voice again sounds through the woods*) *What* on *earth* is that?

CATHERINE

Judge Charlie Cool. . . . that's our signal.

(*She gives the* JUDGE *his answering holler, then climbs up into the tree-house.*)

BARBER

Just like the jungle. . . . Isn't it thrilling? (*Then to* DOLLY, *as though there has been no interruption, and with a relish for his tale*) There you are, my dear—that's what happens when you leave money lying around. And of all people, Verena Talbo. Here we thought she trotted to the bank with every dime came her way. But no. Kept it all in her office safe—didn't *trust* a bank. And so this morning there it was— the door of her safe swung *wide* open. Well, sir, when she saw that she trotted right over to the Lola Hotel, only to discover that her esteemed colleague had checked out—I should say. When they brought her to from her *first* faint, she fainted all over again. Five thousand eight . . .

DOLLY

(*Whirling on* BARBER; *her voice pained, emotional*)

Don't. Don't enjoy misery. Theft. Deceit. I can hear it in your voice—that wretched pleasure. (*She hesitates, it is almost a stutter, then*) Perhaps Verena did not trust the bank. But— I don't know why—she trusted Dr. Ritz. That is what she is suffering—the loss of trust. Once, years ago, my sister loved someone; she doesn't know I know it, but I do. It was Laura

Murphy—maybe you remember her, she worked a while in the post-office. It was a great blow when Laura met that whiskey salesman, married him. I couldn't criticize her . . . It was only fitting if she loved the man. Still, those are the two people I feel Verena has trusted—Laura and—and Dr. Ritz. And both of them—well, it would take the heart out of anyone.

BAKER'S WIFE
(*Sitting down beside* DOLLY)
Never mind Amos, Miss Dolly: he chatters on—but he is your friend, we did come as your friends. And I want to say: come home, Miss Dolly. (*Earnestly, matter-of-factly, and looking directly at* DOLLY, *who is also looking at her*) It sets such a poor example for the town, two sisters quarreling, one of them leaving home in a public manner. Leading citizens have to behave themselves, otherwise the entire place falls to pieces.

BARBER
(*Enthusiastically*)
You should see—crowds like Saturday night. And the Reverend's wife stopping everybody on the street to tell how she's sworn out her own warrant for your arrest because Catherine bit her.

CATHERINE
Bit that old buzzard! I'd be brushing my teeth till doomsday.

BARBER
Oh dear—and I'd so hoped it was true. I do relish a little excitement—though it does make my throat quite dry. I wonder, do you have a drink of water?

(CATHERINE, *in full view of the audience, but in such a manner that the* BARBER *does not see her, begins to fill an empty jelly jar with water from the goldfish bowl.*)

BAKER'S WIFE
(*To* DOLLY; *diffidently*)
And is that your—your tree-house, Miss Dolly?

DOLLY
(*So concentrated she has not heard this question; then, to the* BAKER'S WIFE)
But is she really sick—my sister? I've never known her to be.

CATHERINE
Never a day. (*Handing down the jelly jar of water to the* BARBER) Here y'are, Amos.

BARBER
(*Taking the water from* CATHERINE, *then looking at it with a critical eye, then sipping it*)
Only *where* did it come from? It tastes so sort of—fishy.

CATHERINE
That's just some of Buster's water. (*Nonchalantly wiggling her finger in the goldfish bowl*) Getting mighty shallow in there—huh, Buster?

BARBER
(*Returning the jelly jar to her; icily*)
Thank you.

DOLLY

(*To the* BAKER'S WIFE; *with intense concern*)
But is it *so* what Amos said—about my sister fainting?

BARBER

Verena's not the one to come down with anything an aspirin couldn't fix. I remember when she wanted to rearrange the cemetery, kick everybody out of their graves and put up some kind of fancy mausoleum to house herself and all you Talbos. Poor old Mrs. Twotoes said to me: Amos, don't you think Verena Talbo is the most *morbid* person in town, contemplating such a big tomb for herself? And I said no—the only thing morbid was that she was willing to spend the money when not for an instant did she believe she was ever going to die.

BAKER'S WIFE

I don't know as I think that story is in good taste, Amos. (*Rising*) Before you talk yourself into a grave, kindly lead me back to town. . . .

(*On the words "back to town"* COLLIN *and* MAUDE *and the* JUDGE *enter together from the rear right; they are laughing, as though at some story the* JUDGE *has been telling them.*)

JUDGE

(*As they enter, and with a cheerful flourish*)
No elopement, no elopement. You can rest your soul, Catherine. They just were wading in the river. . . .

CATHERINE

Wading? How? (*She snorts*) Buck-naked?

DOLLY
(*To Catherine*)
Hush now. Now hush. That's not a bit pleasant.

MAUDE
(*Shyly*)
It's God's own truth, Miss Dolly. We were only wading.
(*Then gazing around at the group*) I want to ask a favor of
you all—please don't say to anyone about my being here;
you know how my daddy is. . . .

(*She looks with especial significance at the* BARBER.)

BARBER
(*With a hand to his chest*)
Why roll your eyes at me? Mercy knows, *I'm* no gossip.

COLLIN
Aw, tell her old man. Let him lump it. When I join the
navy, Maude can be one of my dependents.

CATHERINE
(*Drily*)
Well, Dollyheart—looks like we're gonna be living on
less and less.

DOLLY
(*To Maude*)
Don't fret, child. You go along to town with Amos and
Mrs. County.

(MAUDE *nods; helped by* COLLIN, *she gathers and
straps her schoolbooks. The* JUDGE *and the* BARBER,

*mumbling together conversationally, move toward the
grass; they are followed by* DOLLY *and* BAKER'S WIFE.
CATHERINE *remains in the tree-house.*)

BAKER'S WIFE
(*To* DOLLY, *as they walk toward the grass*)
I won't have an easy breath till I know you're safe and
home. (*She stops, faces* DOLLY; *then, quietly, warmly*) We
can't live in trees—maybe some of us would like to, but none
of us can. (*With tender intensity*) Be forgiven. Forgive. (*She
kisses Dolly on the cheek*) Good-bye, dear.

(*Joined by* COLLIN *and* MAUDE, *the* BARBER *and
the* BAKER'S WIFE *exit through the grass.* DOLLY
waves.)

CATHERINE
(*Calling*)
Collin—where you think you headed?

COLLIN
(*As he exits*)
I'm going to walk them far as the road.

CATHERINE
See you get back here without no more wadin'.

(*There is a diminishing of light—as though clouds
were passing overhead. Particularly there is a sense of
shadowiness in the tree where* CATHERINE *sits now
with an invisible quietness.*)

JUDGE
(*Looking up at the sky*)
Clouding over . . . I doubt it will rain, though. (*Lifting his*

100

foot and wiggling his ankle) Rain clouds start a hurting in my ankle.

DOLLY
(*With her back to the* JUDGE)
He stole my sister's money.

JUDGE
(*After a puzzled moment*)
Amos did?

DOLLY
Her friend from Chicago. The Doctor. (*The* JUDGE *emits a low, impressed whistle.* DOLLY *looks at him, then*) Should I go home? . . . Mrs. County thinks so. Be forgiven. Forgive. Except—forgiving—that for me has always meant giving way—losing myself until I don't know I can do what you said we must.

JUDGE
(*Coming toward her*)
What we must . . . ?

DOLLY
Find out who we truly are. That is what you said. More than likely—I would discover that I am no one.

JUDGE
You are very much someone.

DOLLY
(*Smiling sadly*)
A spirit? Well, I think spirits are silly things, ghostly things. (*With a radiant widening of her voice*) I want to

shed—like the leaves that fall and show the eternal shape and person of the tree. I want to be seen as this person—for Verena to see this woman that I am: and if she can forgive her, and be forgiven by her, then that is true and right. . . .

JUDGE

(*Stepping a little back from* DOLLY *and gazing at her as though she were new to him*)

Miss Dolly, would you marry me?

DOLLY

(*With lowered head*)

I told you last night—I have not earned the privilege of giving answers.

JUDGE

(*Puzzled*)

Last night?

DOLLY

(*Blushing*)

Oh—then that isn't what you meant?

JUDGE

I didn't know last night that you were anyone who could be married. I kissed you—(*He gently puts his finger on her forehead, marking the place where he has kissed her*)—but we did not *touch*. Because last night I had not seen—this woman.

(*She lifts her head; they are posed, steadily regarding one another. At this moment* COLLIN *and* MAUDE, *the* BARBER *and the* BAKER'S WIFE *have reappeared in the grass with a silent rush, a sudden starkness.*)

102

BARBER
(*Anxiously*)
May I speak to you a moment, Judge?

(*They meet under the tree for a whispered conference —which* CATHERINE, *leaning over the edge of the tree-house, attempts to overhear.*)

DOLLY
(*Tensely*)
Mrs. County—why have you all come back?

BAKER'S WIFE
(*Approaching her, followed by* MAUDE *and* COLLIN)
Get your things, Miss Dolly: you must leave at once— down to the river and out through the backwoods . . .

COLLIN
We're pretty well surrounded. . . . They've made a kind of horseshoe—with men on either side of the grass—and up on the road, when we got there we saw Big Eddie Stover and the Sheriff. . . .

MAUDE
(*Panicky*)
They've got guns, Miss Dolly. . . .

COLLIN
We had to come back here keeping down low in the grass. There's a full half-circle of them out there—waiting.

DOLLY
(*She turns, walks thoughtfully toward the moss-mound, sits down; then*)
Waiting for what?

COLLIN

For nightfall, I figure. Or maybe more fellows.

> (*A brief silence—the* JUDGE *and the* BARBER *join the grouping around* DOLLY. CATHERINE *is still in the tree-house.*)

JUDGE

(*Quietly*)

Well—you know the situation, Miss Dolly. We can pull out or . . .

DOLLY

(*Looking away from everyone*)

To stay—the *right* to stay—it is mine, as much as my medicine, as much as the tree: I cannot let them take it. (*A pause, then*) But please, the rest of you—it isn't your responsibility.

BAKER'S WIFE

It is that, Miss Dolly. A thing like this, we've all got to see it through. (*As if asking for agreement*) Amos? (AMOS *nods*) Maude?

> (MAUDE *looks for a moment desperate, and then, biting her underlip, nods.*)

JUDGE

(*In a businesslike, and even military manner*)

Now listen to me. I've got a rifle. . . . but you'd better, everybody, get a load of rocks—all you can carry—and sticks. We've got to be able to defend ourselves.

DOLLY

(*As the others scurry about obeying the* JUDGE'S *commands; rising*)

Not rocks. Rocks can hurt people. We mustn't do that.

CATHERINE

What about eggs? Nothing like a good oozy egg. I got way over a dozen here.

JUDGE

All right then—haul yourselves into the tree—scatter out on the branches . . .

(*Chattering as they climb, everyone goes to find his tree-roost.*)

BARBER

I'm *deathly* afraid of heights.

BAKER'S WIFE

(*Who is behind the* BARBER)

Keep on going, Amos. I'll catch you if you fall.

BARBER

One thing I've tried all my life not to be is a *roughneck.*

CATHERINE

(*Like a hawker, and as she dispenses eggs*)

Get your ammunition here. Eggs. Fresh eggs. Get 'em while they last. . . . (*She begins happily to partly hum, partly sing*) "Sister Mary wore three links of chain, ev'ry link was Jesus' name, Oh I ain't gonna grieve, gonna grieve, my Lord, ain't gonna grieve, gonna grieve my Lord, ain't gonna grieve, gonna grieve my Lord, my Lord no more."

(MAUDE *and* COLLIN *shinny out and settle on a far branch.* DOLLY, CATHERINE, *and the* BAKER'S WIFE *are in the tree-house itself. The* BARBER *straddles a branch above the tree-house. The* JUDGE *remains on the ground, pacing.*)

DOLLY
(*To Catherine*)

Sing right out. Let them hear us. (*Then suddenly singing herself*)
"Oh the tallest tree in Paradise
Christians call it the tree of life . . ."

(CATHERINE *joins her, full-voiced*)

"Oh I ain't gonna grieve, gonna grieve my Lord,
Ain't gonna grieve, gonna grieve my Lord,
Ain't gonna grieve, gonna grieve my Lord, my Lord no more."

EVERYONE
(*The next stanza is sung all together; and the lighting, as they sing, dwindles like a slowly deflating balloon*)

"Sister Mary wore three links of chain
Ev'ry link was Jesus' name
"Oh I ain't gonna grieve, gonna grieve my Lord,
Ain't gonna grieve, gonna grieve my Lord,
Ain't gonna grieve, gonna grieve my Lord, my Lord no more."

(*Now the scene is in complete darkness. The voices come up stronger*)

"Oh the tallest tree in Paradise
Christians call it the tree of life . . ."

106

Taken for *Life* by Photographer Cecil Beaton

(*Here, the singing abruptly stops—for a flashlight has sparkled in the dark. Then, to the accompaniment of an acute, stabbing musical sound, other flashlights, spaced at differing angles, pop their light and focus it on the tree. There is a total of seventeen people on stage: the* JUDGE *and those in the tree account for seven of them. The other ten are: the* SHERIFF, *the three men known as* BIG EDDIE STOVER, BROPHY *and* SAM, *and two other men, the* REVEREND, *the* REVEREND'S WIFE *and the* CHOIR MISTRESS—*all of these, except the tenth person, who is* VERENA, *manipulate flashlights. The lights, then, are all centered on the tree.* DOLLY *and her friends blink in the glare: they cannot see who is below them.*)

VERENA
(*From the darkness*)
You fools.

(*The flashlights, in concert with a chilling sentence of music, swerve their beams away from the tree and directly at* VERENA. *She is therefore the only person on stage who is visible. She is dressed in black, is wearing the black hat with the grey dove.*)

THOSE IN THE TREE
(*Together, and with a sudden intake of breath*)
Verena . . .

VERENA
You, Dolly—conniving with these swine to make a mockery of our name.

DOLLY
(*From the darkness*)
Because there are people willing to help each other—you call them swine? If that is what you believe, then our name, your name, deserves to be a mockery.

VERENA
(*Precisely, as though it were a clinical opinion*)
You are not yourself.

DOLLY
(*From the darkness*)
But I am. I've taken your advice: stopped hanging my head, I mean. You said it made you dizzy. And not so very long ago—you told me you were ashamed of me. Of Catherine. So much of our lives had been lived for you—it was painful to realize the waste that had been. Can you know what it is—such a feeling of waste?

VERENA
(*She turns, as though she cannot endure the question Dolly has asked: she seems, with the lights at her back outlining her, an isolated, desolate figure. Then, in a breaking voice*)
I'm not a well woman. I'm sick—I am, Dolly.

(*We hear a rustling sound: It is* DOLLY *descending from the tree, followed by* COLLIN. *Several of the flashlights turn on them and follow their progress; the others stay fixed on Verena, toward whom* DOLLY *goes as though she intended to comfort her. Just as* DOLLY *is within a yard of* VERENA, *two men reach out and seize her. There is, from those in the tree, a shocked gasp, an outcry.*)

VERENA
(*Coming suddenly to Dolly's defense*)
Stop it. . . . Don't touch my sister. . . . Take your hands off her.

THE SHERIFF
(*From the darkness, and in a voice like a long echo*)
It's for the law now, Miss Verena. This is for the law to handle.

(*Another outcry—then, as the two men try to hold onto* DOLLY *and* COLLIN *struggles to free her, tumult: the flashlight beams careen and tangle in the dark. Music parallels these happenings—rises, rises, as though toward a note it can never reach: it is reached in the sound of a gunshot. The gunshot, a hush, at last a young girl's screams. The flashlights sweep the stage and single out, with a frozen steadiness,* COLLIN. *There is a trance-like stillness about the scene—* COLLIN, *with his head strangely cocked to one side, stands confronting the mob.*)

COLLIN
Don't—don't hurt my Dolly.

(*He sways—then, spotted by the flashlights, falls to the ground. As those on the ground converge around him, the darkness lifts a little as if a brilliant moon had begun to rise above them.*)

A MAN'S VOICE
(*From inside the circle around Collin*)
Is he dead?

DOLLY
(*From inside the circle*)
It's Dolly, Collin. Open your eyes, darling. For me . . .

CATHERINE
(*From the tree*)
I never meant a mean word, baby child. I cut out my tongue.

JUDGE
(*From inside the circle*)
Stand back. Everybody—get back.

(*The crowd parts: we see the* JUDGE *and* DOLLY *kneeling by* COLLIN.)

VERENA
Who fired that shot? Which of you idiots?

(*There is a low murmur among the men.* VERENA *snatches the nearest flashlight and casts its beam over the men's downcast faces; she stops on* BIG EDDIE STOVER, *whose plump face sags with fear.*)

BIG EDDIE STOVER
Hell, I never meant to shoot nobody. Was doing my duty, is all.

VERENA
Not all. I hold you responsible, Mr. Stover.

DOLLY
No one is that. No one can be held responsible, except ourselves.

JUDGE

(*To* DOLLY)

We'd better get him to town fast as we can.

(*By now everyone has come down from the tree. The* JUDGE *lifts* COLLIN—*his arms hang down, his head is thrown back;* MAUDE *holds one of his hands. A procession, in which* COLLIN *is the center figure, files past* DOLLY. *The flashlights, focused on the ground, swing like lanterns, and music, a memory of the wind in the grass, accompanies their long exit.* VERENA *does not quite leave the stage: she waits at the edge of the grass for* DOLLY. DOLLY *looks at the tree, bows her head—as the curtain falls, she extends her hands toward the tree in an attitude of rejection.*)

(*Curtain*)

ACT TWO

SCENE II

Later the same evening.

The set is the same as in the first scene of Act One: the exterior of the Talbo house and its dining room. The room is lit by the ruby-glass chandelier and two wall lights; the draperies are drawn, the kitchen door is closed, the door at the left is open.

VERENA *is standing at the windows, her back to the audience: she is slightly holding back the draperies and peering out. The* JUDGE *is seated at the table;* DOLLY *is standing at the other side of it, her hand listlessly, endlessly polishing the frame of a chair.* MAUDE *is seated in a chair against the wall.*

Presently DOLLY *looks up at the ceiling, as if trying to see into the room where* COLLIN *lies. Then she looks at the cuckoo clock.*

DOLLY
(Referring to the clock)
It's stopped again. *(To the* JUDGE*)* What time is it?

JUDGE
(Consulting a pocket watch)
Twelve—a little after. You ought to be home, Maude. You ought to be asleep.

MAUDE
I couldn't anyway. Not without knowing.

113

DOLLY

Go, Maude; it's better that you do. I will send word.

MAUDE

(*Rising, she walks reluctantly toward the door; then, turning*)

Do you think—would Doctor Carter let me see Collin—for only a moment? I want to tell him something. (*She is looking at* DOLLY *and accepts* DOLLY'S *silence as an answer*) Then will you tell him for me—that it's true what I said about thinking of little things; because all I can think is—he must come to my Halloween party. He—must.

> (*She exits. The front door opens, we see* MAUDE *come out carrying her schoolbooks; she gazes for an instant at the upper windows of the house, then exits. Simultaneous with the moment* MAUDE *stands staring at the upper windows,* CATHERINE *enters the dining room; she is carrying a tin washbasin and her sleeves are rolled up. The* JUDGE *quickly rises at her entrance.* VERENA, *for the first time, looks away from the windows and, like* DOLLY, *regards* CATHERINE *with an anxious expression.*)

JUDGE

What does Carter say?

CATHERINE

(*Rather gruffly, and as she sails across the room toward the kitchen door*)

He says for me to fetch him some more hot water. (*She stops in front of the kitchen door, turns back and holds out her hand with the palm open*) There it is. The bullet. (*As she walks back to the table, as she puts it down*) Old Collin was real brave—not one whimper—just let Doc Carter dig it out of him: was here in the shoulder. (*The* JUDGE *reaches for the bullet, as if he wanted to examine it;* CATHERINE *snatches it up*) No you don't. . . . (*As she exits toward the kitchen door*) . . . I'm saving it for that boy to show his children!

> (DOLLY *moves toward the* JUDGE—*still-faced at first, then with a quiet tearful-laughing relief: there is nothing hysterical about this—rather, it is as though she were immensely exhilarated. The* JUDGE *smiles at her, holds her.* VERENA, *observing them woodenly, moves round the table, puts her hand on the back of a chair.*)

VERENA
(*To the* JUDGE, *and with an effort*)

I have something to say to my sister. I could say it more easily if we were alone.

JUDGE
(*Removing his hands from* DOLLY *and placing them in his pockets, then for a moment pondering* VERENA *as though he were trying to read her mind; at last, as if he'd come to a sudden decision*)

I'm afraid you'll have to put up with me, Miss Verena. I have an interest in the outcome of what you might have to say.

VERENA
(*Coldly*)

I doubt that. How so? (*She waits for his reply.* CATHERINE *enters from the kitchen door and, carrying the wash*

*basin filled with steaming water, hurriedly crosses the room
and exits out the dining room door*) How so, Charlie Cool?
(*Then, when there is still no reply forthcoming*) As a man
with a legal background, I'm certain you will appreciate my
coming to the point. Frankly—you're not a welcome sight to
me. My sister could not have gone through with such tommy-
rot if you had not—if some stronger willful spiteful person—
had not been goading her on. So I'll thank you to leave us; it
can be no further affair of yours.

DOLLY

But it is. (*As she sits down in a chair at the table*) Because
Judge Cool . . .

JUDGE

(*Leaning his hands on the table and looking at*
DOLLY)

Dolly means that I have asked her to marry me.

VERENA

(*A brief, disbelieving laugh; then*)

That—is remarkable. Very. I wouldn't have credited either
of you with so much imagination. Or is it that I am imagining? Quite likely I am dreaming—except that I never have
dreams. Or could it be that I only forget them? I suggest this
one we all forget.

JUDGE

I'll own up, Verena. I think it is a dream. But a man who
doesn't dream is like a man who doesn't sweat: he stores up
a lot of poison.

VERENA

(*She has not listened to him; her attention is fixed on* DOLLY. *Then, in a tone of finality*)

I see. You've accepted him.

DOLLY

(*Quietly*)

I thought I would know what was right. But it hasn't happened. Rather, what has happened is—I can see now that in a vain self-pitying corner of myself I've always felt that *I alone* knew what was right. Just as you did, Verena. And people who believe they alone are right can do nothing but deliver ultimatums. You made an ultimatum. It meant we had to leave this house; and in leaving—that was mine to you. And together we made an ultimatum to God; and He answered us—He chose Collin—I don't know why, because that bullet was meant for me. (*Pause; then*) I thought—to have a life made of my own decisions—is that not what we're meant to do?

VERENA

But we have had our lives. Yours has been nothing to despise: you've never been deeply alone, you've never been deeply betrayed. (*A pause, then*) I've envied you always.

DOLLY

Is it true, Judge? Have we had our lives?

JUDGE

Not you. Not me.

VERENA

(*She has not taken her eyes off Dolly, has seemed hypnotized by her. As she comes toward* DOLLY, *as she touches the back of her chair*)

Envied you. I walk through the house—nothing is mine. Your rooms, your kitchen, the house is yours. . . . I can only knock at the door—as I've knocked at the doors of other houses; not often—enough to know that now there is no one but you to let me in. Because Dr. Ritz, Morris—help me, I loved him, I did. It was, oh I admit it, that we were kindred spirits. We looked at each other, we saw the same devil: it was—merry. But he outsmarted me; I'd known he could, and hoped he wouldn't, and he did, and now—(*She begins to slide downward, holding the chair with one hand and with the other fiercely gripping Dolly's wrist*)—it's too long to be alone, a lifetime. Dolly, Dolly—let me live with you, I'm feeling old, I want my sister. (*She is crying, she presses her face against* DOLLY, *who passes a soothing hand over her hair*) You won't leave me?

DOLLY

I won't leave you. (*She looks at the* JUDGE, *who has turned his back on them as though he had no right to be there, as though he wished to make himself invisible. Rising, she starts toward him, stops; then*) Forgive me—I want my sister, too. (*The* JUDGE, *his back still turned, nods. . . . It is as if he does not trust himself to speak; he begins slowly to move toward the door—*DOLLY *takes a step after him, then*) Sometimes—you will come to see me?

> (*The* JUDGE *does not look at her—it is as though he could not bear it if he did; then, with an agonizing nod, and never once glancing back, he exits—immediately appearing again at the front door. He walks across the stage and exits.* DOLLY *has in a sense followed his exit—she has watched him go out the dining room door; then, as he crosses the stage, her whole body gradually turns in the direction of his*

118

Taken for *Life* by Photographer Cecil Beaton

departure. Until he has left the stage there is silence in the dining room. VERENA *has pulled herself up, is standing beside the chair.*)

VERENA
(*As though thinking aloud*)
You've never seen the ocean, have you? (*She waits;* DOLLY *looks at her*) It is a comforting sight—a wave leaving a shell, a wave taking it back. We could go on a trip: the two of us—or Collin and Catherine may come if you like. I've considered selling a few—a few properties. It could be a long trip. We might take a boat. I could show you the ocean.

DOLLY
The ocean? . . . That would only be another tree-house, Verena, something we should not allow ourselves. There is so much to be lived—and my life is here. You were wrong— we've not had our lives.

CATHERINE
(*Appears in the doorway, rolling down her sleeves and with the look of having finished a job; as she enters the room*)
Doc Carter's leaving now—Collin's asleep.

VERENA
(*Softly*)
Please, then, Catherine, turn down the lights.

CATHERINE
(*As she crosses the room to switch off a wall light at the far right; irritably*)
I left Buster, Dollyheart—left him there in the tree. I best go get him 'fore he catches his death.

119

DOLLY

It's not such a cold night. We'll go tomorrow. We must take our spades. . . . I want to get enough dropsy herbs to see us through the winter.

CATHERINE
(*As she moves to switch off another wall light*)
Who's gonna carry all that? You know the worries I have with my back—and Collin, that boy's not gonna be in any condition a while yet. . . .

DOLLY

We could hire somebody. Or take in a new partner. If he would accept—I think we should make the Judge a partner.

VERENA
(*To Dolly—they are several feet apart, at opposite ends of the table*)
May I . . . may I come with you too? I would like to help —if you will let me.

(DOLLY *looks at* VERENA—*starts to go toward her, pauses and holds out her hand; it is a gesture of welcome and, as she lifts her hand, as* VERENA *advances to accept it, music begins. Together,* DOLLY *and* VERENA *move toward the dining room door.* CATHERINE, *watching them, clicks the switch that controls the chandelier. Slowly the chandelier dims; the scrim falls and for a moment, as the music rises, we see it glow, then darken.*)

(*Curtain*)